GYO OBATA ARCHITECT | CLIENTS | REFLECTIONS

GYO OBATA ARCHITECT | CLIENTS | REFLECTIONS

BY MARLENE ANN BIRKMAN
DESIGNED BY KIKU OBATA & COMPANY
EDITED BY HOK AND KIKU OBATA & COMPANY

images
Publishing

Published in Australia in 2010 by
The Images Publishing Group Pty Ltd
ABN 89 059 734 431
6 Bastow Place, Mulgrave, Victoria 3170, Australia
Tel: +61 3 9561 5544 Fax: +61 3 9561 4860
books@imagespublishing.com
www.imagespublishing.com

National Library of Australia Cataloguing-in-Publication entry

Author:	Birkman, Marlene Ann.
Title:	Gyo Obata : architect clients reflections / Marlene Ann Birkman.
ISBN:	9781864703795 (hbk)
Subjects:	Obata, Gyo, 1923–
	Architecture, American.
	Architecture, Modern–20th century.
	Architecture, Modern–21st century.
Dewey Number:	724.7

Designed by Kiku Obata & Company

Edited by HOK and Kiku Obata & Company

Production by The Graphic Image Studio Pty Ltd, Mulgrave, Australia
www.tgis.com.au

Coordinating editor: Robyn Beaver

Pre-publishing services by Mission Productions Limited, Hong Kong

Printed on 157 gsm Neo Matte paper by Paramount Printing Company Limited, Hong Kong

IMAGES has included on its website a page for special notices in relation to this and our
other publications. Please visit www.imagespublishing.com.

"Gyo's buildings project calm, harmony, and balance. They are appropriate in their presentation, and absolutely belong."

—Mike Collins, National Air and Space Museum

AN OPENING: MARLENE ANN BIRKMAN

Since childhood, I marveled at the intricacies of nests, hives, webs, ant hills, leaf houses, snow forts, and sandcastles. I never imagined that one day Gyo Obata would invite me to experience the inner world of architecture and its simple majesty.

"Please call Gyo Obata at HOK—314-421-2000. Thank you." the e-mail read. I was curious. Gyo's late wife, Courtney, and I had visited a week earlier. Greeting me, she, in her inimitable style, escorted me on a narrated tour of their nature-inspired home. Rudy and Petunia, their two Bouviers, tagged along. Then, with a tray and cups, we walked on stepping stones to the nearby barn original to the suburban

...he expressed his desire to write about how buildings evolve because of the architect/client relationship...

property. Restored by Gyo, it has spectacular glass panels and doors which allowed Courtney, an artist, and the family to use it as a studio as well as a gathering space.

Sitting in winter sunlight, sipping our green tea, we laughed together relating antics of our lives. I thanked her for January joy and remarked, "I grew up in Indiana and saw many barns, but this Obata barn redefines the word for me." In no way, except for the russet color, did it resemble vernacular Hoosier architecture. During our easy chatter, Courtney spoke cheerily about Gyo and son, Max, but there was no hint of a book project.

Nine days later, I arrived again at the Obatas' for a meeting with Gyo. In a morning phone call, he expressed his desire to write about how buildings evolve because of the architect/client relationship and wanted to explore the idea. Although I had been introduced to Gyo at social occasions and heard about him when I led an HOK Writing by Design seminar, I did not know him. For years, Gyo anecdotes circulated St. Louis, one being that co-workers daily collected sketches and doodles from his wastebasket after he left work. As a folklore enthusiast, I was intrigued and soon found myself clipping articles about him and HOK .

That Friday, at 4 p.m., Gyo, ever-elegant, welcomed me at the door. Sitting at the dining room table, he got right to the point. In a gentle manner and few words, he described his wish: to write about the human factor in architecture. When he invited me to collaborate, I thanked him. Stunned, I then voiced reasons why I might not be the one. Without flourish, he simply handed me an HOK project booklet and said, "Think about it, and let me know." Later at home, I looked through the red booklet. Five days later, shifting into high gear, I called Gyo and answered, "Yes." Deciding to trust the creative spirit, we set off to see where it would carry us. The one-hour, January 19, 2007, meeting opened a vista.

In February, Gyo and Courtney hosted a Mardi Gras party. Courtney called and simply said, "Why don't you come to dinner on Tuesday." When I saw cars lining the lane, I was surprised. Vivid greens, yellows, and purples decorated the candle-lit barn. A long, rectangular table sat in the center. Thirty-some merrymakers shared the mirth. Except for the Obatas, I knew only two others, the Peppers. As I watched Gyo distribute hand-written place cards, I recalled Dorothy Parker's story *But the One on My Right,* an interior monologue about a dinner party. When I looked for my name, I discovered that I would be seated with Gyo to my right, and thankfully also next to Ted Pepper. At the time, I was slightly nervous around Gyo. Years of reading, as well as hearing about him from HOK seminar participants, lingered.

Inevitably, I dropped my silk napkin. It somehow slid under the table in front of Gyo's feet. After unsuccessful attempts to retrieve it, I decided to do the unthinkable: scoot the chair back and lower my head under the table. Strangely, at that moment, I remembered HOK seminar members commenting that Gyo's socks were "visually excessive." To see if they were teasing, I decided to check. I soon heard Ted Pepper, a physician, say, " Is everything okay down there?" Laughing, I surfaced with the napkin and inquired about Gyo's socks.

At that moment, I began to relax. The ice cracked, and I continued my footwork. I asked Gyo about a favorite place. Without hesitation, he responded, "Michigan." With his right hand, he reached into his pocket and pulled out a small stone. Delighted by his answer and artifact, I asked, "Is that a Petoskey?" He nodded and added, "I try to carry a little piece of Michigan wherever I go." A few weeks later I was flying to Williamsburg to speak at the National Council for History Education Conference. Among other provisions, Courtney brought over a gold, silk fortune cookie. Inside, was a Petoskey stone. I have kept it on my desk ever since.

During April, the Obatas held a family Easter festivity in the barn. Long, pastel ribbons attached to poles fluttered outside in the wind. Eggs, paint, dye, decals, markers, baskets, and candy decorated inside tables. A line-up of marshmallow chicks—a Peeps® display—captured the gaiety. Amidst the revelry, Courtney asked Gyo to cut a large cheesecake. In seconds, I watched him effortlessly and with sure precision slice the dessert. The exactness of the slivers seemed accurate to the millimeter. In that action, I realized why Gyo could so naturally focus on the big picture. Particulars came easily to him; they seemed to be a given. On that Sunday, my knowledge of Gyo took on new dimensions.

In that sunny stillness, I discovered that for Gyo, work seemed without tug or pull. It was concentrated play.

Soon after, I began interviewing Gyo about the projects. Our conversations took place at the house, barn, or office. In July, when the Obatas traveled to Michigan, they invited me to join them for six days. Armed with cell phone, audio recorders, paper, and pens, I envisioned days of productivity, a working vacation. But something happened after Gyo greeted me at the Traverse City airport, and I settled in. I breathed the cool air of Northport, smelled the pines, listened to the ebb and flow of the water, and deflated. After only a day's dose, I understood the lure of Michigan and felt Gyo's affinity with the place.

Gyo typically started his Michigan mornings with a walk. In the afternoon, busy with an outdoor project or reading, he graciously asked, "Do you want to have a session or would you like to take a nap?" Unexpectedly, in the wooded sanctuary, I often opted for a nap; the rhythmic mystery of Lake Michigan did its work. With a knowing smile, Gyo continued sketching a design for a Santa Fe residence on a table in the living room. From the balcony, I often looked down at the bright, natural space dotted with red, yellow, green, and purple pillows on the birch twig furniture designed by Gyo. I watched. With Rudy at his feet and his

Ultimately, the buildings are a reflection of not only the people who shape them, but also of those who make, inhabit, and visit them. Therein lies the ingenuity.

head resting on his left hand, his right hand moved. In that sunny stillness, I discovered that for Gyo, work seemed without tug or pull. It was concentrated play.

During autumn, my exchanges with Gyo resumed at his home and then more often at HOK. One Saturday afternoon, the Obata house was a' bustle with visitors and ringing phones. Gyo and I decided to move our glasses of pomegranate juice and recorders from the dining room into his home office, so that he could reminisce about his life. Reluctantly, I asked if he would try something that he might find strange. In order to call-up details, I wanted

to take him on an excursion using guided imagery. In his fun spirit, Gyo got up from his desk chair and turned off the lights. For two hours, uninterrupted, we sat with our eyes closed talking about his youth. He highlighted places, materials, and landscape. Like all of us, Gyo lives by image; but his glimpses showed that he is an architect at the core. Like writer John Updike in his memoir, *The Dogwood Tree: A Boyhood,* Gyo radiated awareness that place is integral to life itself.

Additional interviews with Gyo occurred at the HOK world headquarters, the seventh floor of One Metropolitan Square, an HOK-designed building in downtown St. Louis. Sophisticated, yet simple, light, and open, its expanse seems unable to contain the imaginations of those who work there. One day as I sat across from Gyo at a conference table near a window overlooking the city, I noticed his focus shift from me to the table. I wondered what he was thinking, knowing, of course, that thinking is what he does. When we stopped for lunch, he left abruptly. He quickly returned with a tape measure. Intently, he began measuring the rectangular table and said, "Just as I thought, three-inches too high, thirty-inches. I will get this table cut down." Weeks later, when I returned, I noticed a difference. Gyo's keen eye and attention to action is immediate, dynamic, and always at work.

Gyo Obata is in no way a quick study. What he says, what he does, what others say about him offer clues, but at heart, he is a creative spirit. Despite his sense of knowing and steadfast nature, he is mysterious. One day I said, "Gyo, a good story demands tension, a collision of the light and the dark. I am looking to you and the clients for conflict, and it seems nonexistent. What can I stir up?" Seemingly removed from the fray, he just looked at me and smiled. As

Gyo radiated awareness that place is integral to life itself.

I left the office, I confirmed, once again, that a visit with Gyo is a visit with the extraordinary.

Gyo exhibits a quiet exuberance for life that is unbounded. He is a "yea-sayer" to gardening, sports, art, travel, reading, dogs, birds, music, theatre, opera, films, politics, construction, television, cooking, friends, and family. For him, each instant is a singular one, special to that moment. Each project is a distinct one, unique to the requirements, client, and site. Each building presents a new problem ready to be solved.

Collectively, Gyo's clients and associates reveal a composite picture of him, the creative process, and the projects. Along with Gyo, they are in word and deed, the people behind the principles that shaped the beauty and function of the buildings. But they are only a part of that picture. Ultimately, the buildings are a reflection of not only the people who shape them, but also of those who make, inhabit, and visit them. Therein lies the ingenuity.

Early in the project, I asked Gyo to write his name in Japanese. When he completed the characters, he explained that "Gyo" means "dawn" and "Obata," "little field." What I discovered is that Gyo Obata is living his name, one thoughtfully given to him with love by his parents Chiura and Haruko. His appellation is his hallmark.

Inherent to his design philosophy is light ("dawn") and site ("little field"). Gyo elaborates, "The language that architects use to define space is daylight. Each project offers new potential for discovery, for understanding the site and program, and an opportunity to do a thoughtfully designed building that will bring meaning and enjoyment to the people who will occupy it." His name captures the essence, the spirit of his work which spans the globe and two centuries.

Gyo is a family member of 18 generations of artists. His light is evident in his being and buildings. Timeless and ageless, Gyo Obata, the person and architect, moves forward with grace and optimism. For him, each day is an opening, a portal to possibility.

"Each project offers new potential for discovery, for understanding the site and program, and an opportunity to do a thoughtfully designed building that will bring meaning and enjoyment to the people who will occupy it." —Gyo Obata

A Postscript

Visitors enter the Obata home on a mosaic stone path designed by Courtney. One row is a line of Petoskeys, fossilized coral. According to folklore, the pebbles were named after Petosegay, a fur trader who achieved distinction for his tribe. "Petosegay" means "rising sun," "rays of dawn," or "sunbeams of promise."

During the summer, visitors at the Obata home see morning glories ablaze in Gyo's garden. He soaks the seeds, puts them in starting pots, tends the sprouts, and then carefully plants them. True to his nature, in any season, indoors or outdoors, Gyo is always close to the earth.

Reference
http://www.deq.state.mi.us/documents/deq-ogs-gimdl-GGPS.pdf

BIOGRAPHY: **GYO OBATA**

1923
Gyo Obata is born in San Francisco
to Chiura and Haruko Obata

I was born in San Francisco in 1923 to two artists, Chiura Obata, a painter, and Haruko Obata, a floral designer who introduced Ikebana School to the West Coast. Our house was like a studio, and was always filled with paintings and flowers. My parents were both great teachers and taught me life's most basic lesson: to listen very carefully.

When I was five years old, I traveled to Japan on a boat with my family. I have vivid memories of my paternal grandmother's house in Sendai. From the street, I saw a fence. I entered a little forecourt and came into a stone-covered area where I took off my shoes. I stepped up into the main part of the house, which had clean straw tatami mat floors. The house was simple and heated with charcoal in the hibachi. When we were cold, we hovered around it and talked. At night, my grandmother brought out big blankets and we slept on the floor. Everything always seemed in place and in proper proportion. The house had a remarkable feeling of privacy and serenity.

I clearly remember the beautiful shoji screens—rice paper pasted onto rectangular wooden slats, all sliding doors. Outside of the shoji, there was a bamboo sliding door that we closed at night. During the day, it was opened so that we could see into the back of the house, where we looked into the garden—an elegant Japanese garden.

When we returned home to San Francisco, I started grammar school. My mother placed me in a school away from the Japanese section of town. She did not want to send me to a segregated school with all Japanese-

Americans. My classes in Redding were held in a compact urban building. Our playground was on the roof. One other boy and I were the only Japanese-American students. I did not feel different.

When I was in the fourth grade, we moved to Berkeley. My father became a teacher at the University of California Art School. We rented a free-standing house that had a large garden in back with lots of shrubbery, flowers, and trees. The contrast was incredible to the dense, three-story walkup that had been our San Francisco home in the heart of Japan Town. I remember thinking, "We must be out in the woods."

In sixth grade, my teacher asked what each student aspired to be. I responded, "I want to be an architect." My mother once said that architecture was not only about art, but also about science and engineering and that it was a good profession.

For me, school was all about studying. In my family, it was clearly understood that the second generation had to come home with straight As. Also, as a Japanese-American, I had no social life. Although I had very good relationships with my classmates during elementary, junior high, and high school, after school there were no social engagements. We were not allowed to mix. So, I studied hard and got good grades.

The summers excited me because our family's dear friends, the Kodanis, founded a fishing village in Point Lobas. I spent a month living with them and wandering through Point Lobas Park, which is now a state park. On other vacations, our whole family spent time in Yosemite, where my father taught with renowned photographer Ansel Adams. My father really liked the beauty and

LEFT Gyo Obata, 1927
RIGHT Haruko and Chiura Obata, 1913

1941
University of California
Berkeley, California

1945
Washington University, St. Louis, Missouri
Bachelor of Science in Architecture

tremendous scale of Yosemite, and did a lot of landscape paintings. I often invited friends along. In Yosemite, we hiked the trails and delighted in the waterfalls. We slept outside in sleeping bags and in tents when it rained.

From high school, I entered the School of Architecture at Cal. The building itself looked interesting. It was stepped up the hillside; the freshmen were on the high level. As students advanced in the program, they moved closer to the ground and to the library. We began with 150 students in the program, and at the end of our freshman year, only 30 remained. They used a course called Architecture I to weed out students who were not totally committed. In that class, we had to create a detailed composition of an object, which faculty members then judged. I placed first.

Cal worked us very hard. We started first with pencil drawing and then used black ink. That was good training to get disciplined and understand that architecture takes a lot of effort. The rigor was similar to medical school. The teachers went out of their way to make students work.

I studied all the time. In December 1941, when World War II began, I was in my second year. I never paid attention to the war. Pearl Harbor came on a Sunday and we went to class on Monday. It was a gloomy, rainy, dark day.

Even when we had blackouts, I ignored the war. Tension mounted. People became afraid that the Japanese would invade the West Coast. Then signs appeared on every telephone post in Berkeley, on every block, that said that anybody who had Japanese ancestry needed to be at a certain place by a certain date. They had a week's time to get rid of all their belongings and were only allowed to bring a single suitcase. People of Japanese ancestry in the three West Coast states of Washington, Oregon, and California were to be sent to internment camps.

We had to give up everything, and it was impossible for us to travel without permission. That was when my father said, "You have to get out of here." He heard that if I had an acceptance from a university, I could go to it. I sent a telegram to Dean Langsdorf in charge of Architecture and Engineering at Washington University in St. Louis, Missouri. He replied with an acceptance and, with some difficulty, I received permission to travel east. I was 19 years old.

I left for St. Louis by train the night before my family was taken by bus and moved to a race track called Tanforan, where they were put up in horse stalls with public toilets outside. When I arrived in St. Louis, I did not feel the war at all. It was as if night had become day. The architecture students at Washington University treated me like everybody else, and in good-natured fun, nicknamed me Stub.

In December, the government gave me special permission to visit my family in the internment camp as a free person. From the racetrack, where they stayed three or four months, they were transported to Topaz in Provo, Utah, where the elevation was high. There, they were all put in a little 15' by 15' tar-paper shack. Behind barbed wire, soldiers with machine guns walked around. It was just like a concentration camp. At the camp, my father set up an art school for all the professionals.

During the visit, I remember playing football. But mostly, I remember the feeling of being a free person coming from the outside. Afterwards, I returned to my studies at Washington University and went to summer school, so I could get through the five-year program in four years.

LEFT Gyo in the Army, 1946

ABOVE RIGHT Gyo at work, 1948
RIGHT Gyo Obata and Harry Schulke, 1949

1946
Cranbrook Academy of Art, Bloomfield Hills, Michigan
Master of Architecture & Urban Design

1946–1947
Served in the U.S. Army

1947–1951
Skidmore, Owings and Merrill
Chicago, Illinois

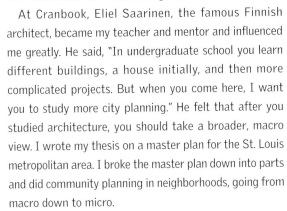

My father always told others, "If you are interested in knowing if we are loyal to the United States or to Japan, just ask. Send the ones who are loyal to Japan to camp. If you are second generation, you are an American citizen and you have to be loyal to your country." At that time, Teddy Roosevelt's Exclusion Act prohibited Asians from becoming citizens of the United States. My father said that he could not give up his Japanese citizenship because that was all he had. But, he told my family that the second generation had to be loyal to the United States.

There was a small group in the camps called Kibei, second generation Japanese born in the United States and sent to Japan to go to school. They disagreed with my father's position on second-generation loyalty and attacked him with an iron bar, damaging his sight. My brother appealed to camp authorities to bring the assailants to justice. They refused. But, because of my father's injuries, the officials let my family leave the camp. Always optimistic, my family never looked back.

The Congregational Church in Webster Groves, Missouri, was very helpful in relocating my family. They found a house on Summit Street and we rented it. My father arrived first and soon after that, my mother, sister Yuri, brother Kim, and his wife followed. My father, mother, and brother worked at an advertising agency. Then Kim started his own commercial art firm, Obata Studio. He did a lot of work for Emerson Electric and Anheuser-Busch, and later launched Emerson's Asian office, and became successful in Tokyo.

When the war ended, my father was invited back to Cal. In 1945, after almost three years in St. Louis, my family returned to Berkeley. I graduated from Washington University and went on to graduate school at Cranbrook Academy of Art in Bloomfield Hills, Michigan, a suburb of Detroit.

At Cranbook, Eliel Saarinen, the famous Finnish architect, became my teacher and mentor and influenced me greatly. He said, "In undergraduate school you learn different buildings, a house initially, and then more complicated projects. But when you come here, I want you to study more city planning." He felt that after you studied architecture, you should take a broader, macro view. I wrote my thesis on a master plan for the St. Louis metropolitan area. I broke the master plan down into parts and did community planning in neighborhoods, going from macro down to micro.

Saarinen was a quiet, soft-spoken individual with beautiful suits. I learned a great deal from him about overall planning, large-scale planning, and detailing. He emphasized the relationship of every element in a design, from the smallest through the largest, and the importance of integrating them. He used to say, "Architectural design begins with a single chair within a room, that expands into a series of rooms, that makes a house, that fits within a group of houses, that creates a neighborhood, that encompasses a town or city."

Cranbrook prepared me to take a broader view, so large-scale planning never frightened me. Since then, I have always been interested in working on large-scale projects where many smaller parts must fit into the

ABOVE LEFT Minoru Yamasaki and Gyo, 1952
LEFT Haruko and Chiura Obata

ABOVE RIGHT Nori, Kiku, Gen and Gyo Obata, 1959

1951–1955
Hellmuth, Yamasaki and Leinweber
Detroit, Michigan

1955
Established Hellmuth, Obata & Kassabaum
Founding Partner

greater whole. Saarinen always asked, "What's the next relationship? What's the connection?" From him, I learned the most valuable lesson for an architect: always look at the next relationship.

After earning a master's degree from Cranbrook, I was drafted into the United States Army and sent to Adak, the biggest port in the Aleutian Islands. They used to say that in the Aleutian Islands, there was a girl behind every tree. But there weren't any trees. It was all tundra grass. When the weather changed, it would meet on the island and we would have 100-mile-per-hour storms. All the buildings were buried in the ground like Quonset huts. Every day we would go out in the cold field to test equipment and clothing. Every night we sat in our hut throwing our combat boots at the rats.

Soon the war ended and I came home. Upon my return from service, Saarinen invited me to work for him, but I chose Skidmore, Owings and Merrill (SOM) in Chicago because I had been in Michigan for two years. At SOM, I had a good experience working on a variety of projects and learned to work quickly.

Around that time, Minoru Yamasaki was working with George Hellmuth and Joseph Leinweber. They started a

firm in Detroit called Hellmuth, Yamasaki and Leinweber. In 1951, Yamasaki invited me to be his assistant. I joined the firm in Detroit, but I spent most of my time in St. Louis, heading up the airport design with Yamasaki. Hellmuth, who had a lot of political connections in St. Louis where he grew up, also traveled there to try to get projects for the Detroit firm. His political friends told him that St. Louis work stayed in St. Louis.

In 1955, Yamasaki wanted to close the St. Louis office because of his health problems. It was at that time that George Hellmuth, George Kassabaum, and I decided to open our own office in St. Louis—Hellmuth, Obata & Kassabaum. Initially our practice was almost entirely in education—elementary and secondary schools. We decided to refocus our practice and diversify by working on as many building types as possible. We enriched our practice to include planners, landscape architects, programmers, interior designers, engineers, graphic artists, and others. And we began to expand the geographic scope of our practice. Now, we have 23 offices: 12 in the United States and 11 out of the country with a total of 2,000 employees.

During the 1970s, there was a recession in architecture. George Hellmuth decided we should go after projects overseas, particularly in Saudi Arabia. We were fortunate to be selected to design the King Saud University and the King Khaled Airport in Riyadh. This experience gave us the understanding of how to practice out of our own country. The core of my philosophy as an architect and as a person stems from my earliest lessons as a boy: listen very carefully, understand what people want, work hard, and find the best ways to enhance the quality of life around you.

ABOVE LEFT Gyo and Courtney Obata
LEFT Gyo in his garden, 1983

ABOVE RIGHT Gyo and Max Obata, 1988
RIGHT Gyo and Courtney Obata, 2005

Gyo Obata embodies everything that's honorable about the architectural profession. Instead of designing for the fashions of the times or to make a personal statement, Gyo designs to improve lives. Imagine that.

Gyo does not have a signature design style. You would never look at a building and say, "That's an Obata." But if you talk to his clients, they will tell you their building fits them like a glove.

Knowing Gyo—my friend and mentor for the past half-century—has been one of the best things that ever happened to me. He is a kind, thoughtful man who is easy to work with and who develops warm, personal relationships with colleagues and clients. People believe in him, which is an essential part of turning drawings into buildings.

Our firm's design philosophy emerges directly from Gyo's vision that architects should listen to clients, work hard, and solve their problems with imaginative yet simple solutions.

"If you listen closely," he would say, "clients will tell you what they really want." It sounds so easy.

For years we have witnessed Gyo's philosophy come to life in every line he has drawn and in his every interaction with clients. His genuine desire to help the world by designing socially conscious, sustainable buildings has transformed countless lives and made me eternally proud to be part of the HOK family. Gyo speaks softly but carries a big legacy.

Today's world is crying out for help. Fortunately, Gyo has guided our firm to a position from which we're truly able to help. This is incredibly rewarding for all of us at HOK. In return for this gift, we have one simple message: Thank you, my friend.

Bill Valentine, FAIA
Chairman, HOK

CONTENTS

This collection of 30 projects and the people connected with them highlight the human factor in architecture.

THE PROJECTS

Gyo Obata,
a founding partner
of Hellmuth, Obata
and Kassabaum or HOK,
delights in design.

"As an architect practicing for more than 50 years, I understand how buildings can contribute to a pleasant or not so pleasant experience for people. I have learned about clear movement through buildings and how important daylight is to bring a space to life. The relationship to the outdoors and nature is so important and, at last, we are finally into sustainability." —Gyo Obata

Excitement comes with packing for a trip, traveling to an unknown place, meeting new people, and waking each day. Beginnings, entrances, openings, and awakenings call up momentum, memory, and meaning. These are often shared with others, but they are always unique to each individual.

Architect Gyo Obata believes that architecture starts with designing for a single person. According to Obata, "Without a client, no building exists, so the relationship between the architect and client creates interesting stories about how buildings become realities. Architecture is about people in spaces and places, so the human factor of the client and the architect is an important part of how these projects develop."

Gyo Obata delights in design. He values his relationships with clients. He elaborates, "I have met so many interesting clients who have given me the responsibility to do their designs, so I hope this book shows how these buildings evolved. There is a saying that if the building is good, it is because the client is good."

Through selected project images and personal reflections of Gyo, his clients, and associates, you are invited to step through thresholds and discover the creative spirit at work and at play. Look and listen, with wonder or curiosity, at moments that shape, connect, and transform lives. Enjoy the journey!

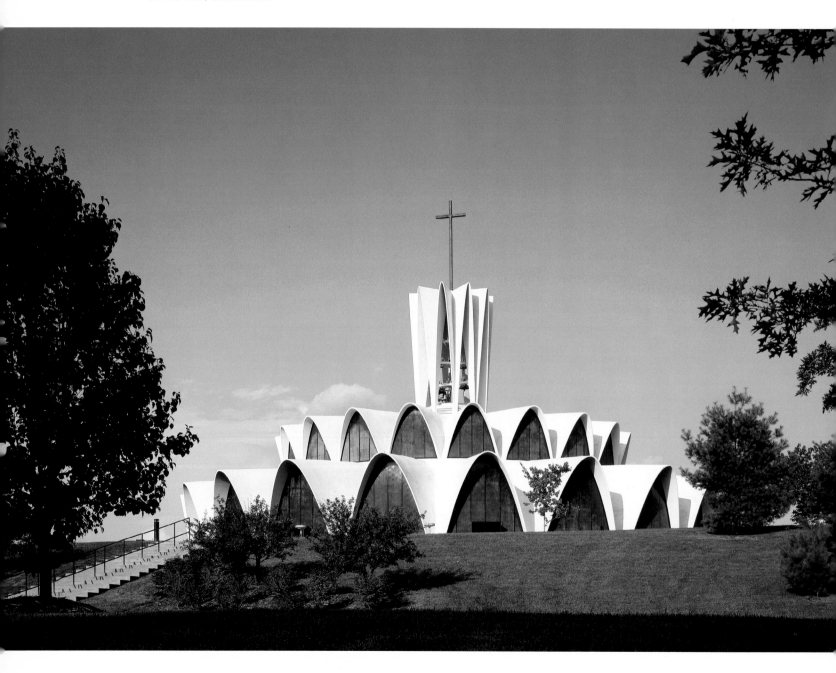

GYO OBATA: A SIMPLE BUILDING IN WHICH TO WORSHIP

I was delighted to work with people excited to create a new, light, airy, and serene

abbey that mirrors the transcendence of spiritual life.

My partner, George Hellmuth, a Roman Catholic, had friends who wanted a new St. Louis Catholic boys school offering the highest standards of scholarship. They visited Ampleforth Abbey, a monastery and preparatory school for boys in Yorkshire, England. The group then invited three monks to come to St. Louis to set up a school: Father Luke, Father Timothy, and Father Columba.

The Oxford- and Cambridge-educated monks came out of a Gothic tradition. Yet, they wanted a fresh beginning and felt that the church and school should reflect a contemporary design. They asked for a series of side chapels (at that time, the monks said the masses individually), a central nave with the altar in the middle for regular services, and a bell tower, which is a Benedictine tradition. These requirements inspired the three layers of arches.

Father Columba wanted famous Italian structural engineer Pier Luigi Nervi to review my studies. Nervi came to St. Louis and I presented the sketches—several different schemes, all round chapels. He recommended the one with parabolic arches, which I also favored, as the best from a structural standpoint.

McCarthy Brothers was interested in contracting but hesitant to bid, given the radical design and its potential costs. Paddy McCarthy figured out how to build the project by constructing a series of wood frames out of plywood, then applying dry cement on a very steep slope. Without the builder's tenacity, our idea would not have taken shape.

Concrete gave the building form. I used thin-shell concrete, which had to be poured very dry or it would just slip off. Instead of stained-glass windows, I found an affordable material called Kalwall®, composed of two plastic surfaces. From the outside, the windows look dark because the outer layer is dark gray. From the inside, they're white. They look like a shoji screen.

In a structure like this, I wanted to contain worshippers within the space so they were not distracted by the visual things outside. Worshippers are surrounded by the arches and feel as though they are totally in another kind of environment. I designed everything to be absolutely as simple as possible. From the wooden pews to the tile floor, everything was kept to an absolute minimum.

It is actually a very simple building. People go inside and it is just one big space. Only two very simple materials are on the inside: tile floors and the plaster. On the outside, it is just the concrete. There is an integrity in the building, the concrete, and the structure.

LEFT Building the Abbey was a challenge and test of faith
RIGHT Wood frames and plywood were forms for the concrete arches

FR. JEROME LUKE RIGBY: A MODERN CHURCH FOR THE NEW WORLD

We had a group of Romanian architects visit on a tour of buildings in the United States. Only one man among them spoke English. He hung back as they moved on and said to me in very broken English while looking up at the church, "Gothic arches in three dimensions." I thought that was a very, very perceptive comment.

The three of us who came here from overseas—Father Columba, Father Timothy, and I—wanted a contemporary church. That rather shocked people in St. Louis, who expected a beautiful Old English-style thing with ivy creeping up the walls, and everything would be good, traditional English architecture. They were a marvelous group and very gracious and trusting of our decision.

Abbot Herbert Byrne told me he wanted me to be in charge of the business end—the money and building construction. Fred Switzer said to me, "You and your partners have got to be very economical as you open this

school because we are raising money to start an institution, but we have nothing to show. We have no building and only a few desks, but we do have the property." Brothers Jerry and Dayton Mudd in fact gave us the church. Their father was the first accountant for a small, growing firm in Wisconsin called J.C. Penney.

We went far and wide looking at architects, but knew there would be an enormous advantage to having a local architect. When we saw the St. Louis airport and the Planetarium, we thought: here is a man on "the cutting edge." So we talked to Gyo. Unlike other architects we had interviewed, Gyo was more interested in listening to us. That made a big impression even though he'd never designed a church. The three of us all agreed—we wanted Gyo Obata.

Father Columba told Gyo that the church would be for boys, who mostly take things in visually. While in church, it would be important for the boys to see what was going on and to have the sense of raising heart and mind up to God. We wanted height, space, and everything to be visible. And we wanted it to cost the average amount for a church that size.

Gyo showed several designs and he explained how Italian engineer Pier Luigi Nervi, who built the Olympic Stadium and Rome's new railroad station, was designing structures with thin-shell concrete. It happened that Nervi

LEFT Side chapels, central nave, and bell tower as seen from the air
RIGHT The arches open the building to admit significant natural light

was going to be in Chicago, and so we asked him to come review our designs. He came, and in a matter of minutes spoke, "There is the one!"

We then had to submit our design plan to St. Louis County. When they saw it, they said, "That will fall down." They insisted we put extra steel in, or they couldn't issue the permits to build the church. The structure now has three times the steel it needs.

The project went smoothly, in the beginning. Gyo worked mostly with Father Columba. I had the client role in the relationship. During the building process, I realized Gyo was listening. We wanted the choir section to be slightly cut off, but not completely. We did not want to break the fullness. On several Sunday afternoons, I found Gyo just sitting in church, trying to figure out what we needed for that space. He said, "Let me hear what Emil Frei has to say." Emil Frei's organization then had a voice in the church interior.

Gyo was a gentleman, a gentle man, and a real listener. He grappled with problems quietly and never made snap decisions. He would take a problem away, think about it, and return having translated our general vision into several possibilities. He would say, "How do you like this?"

Our contractor, McCarthy Brothers, was easy to work with and got along well with Gyo. At one point, they had to replace a heavy machinery operator. They sent out an elderly man who requested to have some practice. He got into the crane and started picking the bell tower up from the ground. After raising it a certain height, the crane would move forward because it was too heavy. So he had to find out how far he could push it across. He did this for a few minutes and then said, "I'm ready." He picked the thing up and he put it down as though he was placing a teacup onto a table. He just put it down, right in the middle of where he wanted it to be. This demonstrated to me that when a building goes up, there are a lot of experts in little areas.

I think we have one of the great churches in the United States. I have yet to hear of anybody in the church say, "I wish we had something different." The project went smoothly. Gyo absorbed information and technology. He absorbed the concepts placed before him and designed our church. I used to tell Gyo he ought to pay us for making him famous by building this church. This was a project full of first-time people who built something completely new. We believed in the project and each other.

Father Jerome Luke Rigby, Order of Saint Benedict, came from the Ampleforth Abbey in England to the United States with Father Timothy and Father Columba to establish a school. Father Luke was the designated Business Manager and Procurator. He is a Prior at the Abbey of Saint Mary and Saint Louis.

FR. GREGORY MOHRMAN: INSPIRING FOR LIFE

We have a story in the monastery of when our founding abbot from England first came here to St. Louis after the church had been built. He saw it and said that it was a "song in concrete."

The first time I ever came into this church was when it was under construction, and I was about 5 years old. I have a vivid memory of coming into the space. The windows were installed, and the pews and the tile hadn't been put in yet. I remember being absolutely blown away by this building. Shortly after it was completed, my father, who had a great devotion to the monks, would come here for mass every Sunday. I came with him, so essentially I have attended this church since I was about 5 or 6 years old.

I went to school here as a student and prayed in this church week-in and week-out, during the school year. After I left school and went to the university, I became a monk. I have prayed in this church five times a day for the last 28 years of my life. I figure I must have come into this building several tens-of-thousands of times throughout all those years. I think the most amazing thing about it for me is that every time I walk into this building, it takes my breath away. I feel as if I'm coming into it for the first time. It's never, ever gotten old. And I've never gotten used to it. I think that's the mark of a truly remarkable building.

This is the church I've prayed in all my life. Its evocation of the transcendence of God in the midst of simplicity of form and subtlety of color and light has always spoken to me very powerfully of the reality of who God is. In many ways, it formed my own vocation to become a monk because it speaks so powerfully of the deep spirituality of monastic life. This building had such an impact on my life because of its form, shape, sound, and the way light enters into it and plays on its surfaces day-in and day-out, season after season.

It strikes me that a really powerful architectural form has the ability to affect and inspire a person's life. If people walk into a space a thousand times and that space still impacts them like it did the very first time, then it has a powerful effect on how they relate to it. It shapes them somehow. I think that's the real power of great architecture. It touches something in human beings that evokes in them a sense of the transcendent. It lifts them

LEFT Simplicity and subtlety are conducive to prayer, meditation, and worship

up and gives them a sense of the purpose, meaning, and beauty in life that informs their growth and their character.

This building does that for thousands of people. There's a parish here. People come here to mass every Sunday. There's a school here for boys from the ages of 12 to 18. They're shaped by the experiences they get in this building over the course of the years they spend here. That's a remarkable gift that the architect gave to us in this space he designed for us.

I come into this building every morning at about half past 5 to pray with the other monks. From that moment of the morning until about 6 or 7 in the evening, I return to this building several times each day to pray. When I go to work over at the school, I walk by it. Bells ring every half-hour all through the day. Each time we look out a window in our monastery, we're impressed by the shape of the building. It's a constant reminder to me of the central part of my life, which is the call to seek God. I don't know of any more powerful symbol to have to call me constantly back to that fundamental vocation, because I can't look at this building without knowing it's about God. For me, it's a powerful image of how God is constantly at work in my life, and in the lives of others.

Father Gregory Mohrman, Order of Saint Benedict, is the Prior of the monastery at the Saint Louis Abbey, and Chaplain of The Saint Louis Priory School.

GYO OBATA: ON A PEDESTRIAN CAMPUS

The design of a university is about the movement of students from classroom to classroom and building to building with limited time between classes. The site's natural beauty is integral to the plan. You must find relationships, trace them through shifting dimensions of time, and come at last to deciding, choosing, committing, and planning. It is a campus as art with natural landscape and a natural site.

At the project's onset, Southern Illinois University (SIU) was in Carbondale and the president was Delyte Morris, an amazing educator. He knew how to work the state of Illinois' political system. Delyte wanted a new university outside of St. Louis on the Illinois side. He got the funding and built a new university.

I was interviewed by Delyte and his staff and got the job. Delyte held a big Environmental Planning–Edwardsville Campus Conference under a plastic dome in East St. Louis. He invited Earl Bolton of the University of California at Berkeley, R. Buckminster Fuller of SIU, Edmund Bacon of Philadelphia, Hideo Sasaki of Harvard, Paolo Soleri of Arcosanti, and Sybyl Moholy-Nagy, the wife of the famous head of Illinois Institute of Technology Institute of Design (previously New Bauhaus School of Design). I spoke about what I thought the potential was, but I was mainly there to listen.

After the conference, Delyte assembled about 2,600 acres on the bluffs of Edwardsville above the Mississippi River. He had some strong design ideas. He did not want any natural light in the classrooms because he wanted people to concentrate. And, he wanted every space to be flexible, including labs that could change from physics, to biology, to chemistry. I had to think through elements like acoustics and movability with engineers. I put all of the fixed elements, such as elevators and stairways, into towers in brick. The flexible areas were the classrooms with the precast concrete walls.

We configured the campus to be a commuter campus. I designed an entire central quadrangle, the university's center, the student center, the library, the administration building, an auditorium/theatre, and the classrooms. We had a good landscape architect, Sasaki, working closely with the site. Because it was a totally pedestrian campus, I placed the major buildings in the central quadrangle. The building construction used only three materials: brick, precast concrete panels with a special aggregate from Colorado, and glass with aluminum frames.

Throughout the years, Southern Illinois University Edwardsville has grown to be a major university. Delyte Morris was a strong leader with strong ideas. He left a tremendous legacy in Edwardsville and Carbondale.

ERIC B. BARNETT: MOVING PEOPLE THROUGH ART

I see it very much as a garden. It is organized like a garden and has the same

effect on me personally as a garden.

I am the director of the University Museum at Southern Illinois University Edwardsville. In June 1968, I came here as an undergraduate, and have pretty much been here ever since. The vision for this project depends on who is telling the story. There are different visions and some of them are very competitive. A big part of the discussions was how we were going to deal with traffic patterns and the movement of people. President Morris started preliminary planning on all this and had a notion of shapes and materials.

Buckminster Fuller wanted to take a very large dome and isolate the academic environment physically from the rest of the world. He pulled this off at the South Pole stations. The dome serves mostly as a windbreaker; it also serves to separate this built environment from the natural environment. That was one idea Bucky had for this campus. It did not happen, but the idea of clustering the buildings and surrounding them with parking did happen.

Some people thought we should ban cars from the campus, have people park on the perimeter, and use transportation systems, like moving walkways, into campus. There was even an idea of creating a rapid transportation system on campus. We do have a couple of old St. Louis/Springfield interurban railroad right-of-ways that go through campus, so it could still happen.

Some of the environmental planners felt we were too accommodating to automobiles. They wanted cars even further away from the core of the buildings. We wound up with parking lots that surround a cluster of buildings, and then beyond the lots are the forests; so we combine the natural environment, the unbuilt environment, and the built environment—drawing people to the center of campus.

While they were planning this whole campus, they were also modeling the shape of the ground. These are not natural formations. We see the bluffs on the west side, but as people come in from the south, they come up over a rise to discover the building. That rise was sculpted to create a sudden "aha!" moment, which is really part of the whole Zen aesthetic. Most people look at rolling hills like that and think, "Oh, that's natural." No, that was manufactured in order to create that aesthetic moment. I think that probably came about because of a conversation with Gyo and the landscape architect. Even before they started the construction process, they had in the back of their minds how they would create that moment.

During one of the iterations of the campus plan, Gyo convinced the architects for the engineering building to move the whole thing 16 feet to the east and a few feet to the north. They had not broken ground on it yet, and moving it would create a space for a museum building and a quad by aligning the engineering building and art building. I thought, "Oh, okay, we'll just relocate the building." It was only a few feet, but it made all the difference.

One of the other elements we focused on was the concept of making art a part of everyone's daily experience on campus. So the interiors of the buildings are very simple and many of the proportions are based on the Japanese math proportions. We have placed artwork from a wide variety of cultures in the buildings because the simplicity of the interior spaces lends itself to this exposition of artwork. That was intentional. It grew out of the ideas of André Malraux, the French Minister of Culture, in the late 1950s and early 1960s, who wanted to remove physical

RIGHT Schematic design of the campus layout shows a central quad

and psychological barriers between people and art. We realized that even the threshold of going into a museum space is a psychological barrier for people.

In most museum collections, we do our best to isolate our exhibits so that people cannot come in direct contact with the objects. Here, we installed things that are very accessible. People can walk up and touch them. It is good from a teaching and learning point of view, but horrible from a conservation point of view. We have artwork in all the public areas, offices, reception areas, faculty offices, and grounds. It is really spread out.

We began with a core of objects that was purchased while the buildings were still under construction. Katherine Kuh, a curator of the Art Institute of Chicago and then an art critic for the *Saturday Review*, was given funds to acquire artwork for the campus. She bought a lot of drawings and prints because they were cheaper than sculpture, but she arranged for some donations of paintings and sculpture. We did buy a Rodin just before the first building opened. Since then we have added to and diversified our collection. Ours is now an encyclopedic collection and we try to support academic programs throughout the university. We have rocks and minerals, shells and fossils, and Native American, Pre-Columbian, African, and other cultural artifacts. We have embraced diversity as a society.

When we were working on planning for a museum building with Gyo and his staff, it became clear to me that in developing a program statement one must deal with functionality and allow the architect to deal with developing that functionality. One thing that really upsets architects is for the client to show them a lot of clippings out of magazines and architecture books. They think you are trying to design your own place. But if you know what the functions are, what functions need to be adjacent to others, and how things need to be sequenced, then the job of the architect is to create the form.

Gyo is good about getting people to express the functions they want. He has the calm and quiet that comes from knowing. I have seen people try to create that impression, but they do not have the inner tranquility that he possesses. I am sure it came from a whole set of life experiences that would have broken some people. Gyo never had to demand respect; it flows to him naturally. He listens before he starts showing ideas. I learned from one of the women who worked at HOK that he doodles and throws his doodles away. People at the office used to follow him around and take them out of the trash cans so they could have an archive of his thought process.

ABOVE Students and faculty enjoy the pleasing, accessible open spaces
LEFT Art installations throughout the campus invite daily contact with art

LEFT The campus is enhanced by a Zen-garden influenced landscape plan

Throughout the years, a lot of modifications have been made to the buildings because the original purpose was modified or changed. One example is the Communications Building, now Dunham Hall. When it was built, the theatre space in that building was designed to accommodate television productions. The plan was to have another building next to it that would have a performing arts theatre. Well, that second building never got built and the space had to go through a series of modifications to make it fit the functionality.

In the Rendleman Building, every time a new chancellor or vice chancellor is hired, remodeling occurs. Several years ago, they had two new vice chancellors at the same time. They had suites of offices on the second floor and were both reconfiguring their offices and redesigning their suites. They did not talk to each other; they just did what they wanted to do. They had an area that neither one of them took and so they walled it off, but there were no doors. So the guys in facility management built it the way it was drawn. Only later did one of the vice chancellors wonder what was on the other side.

When the campus was first conceived, one of the goals was to accommodate the academic needs of the people in the metropolitan area who would not otherwise have an opportunity to go to college. Gradually, we are moving away from being a 100 percent commuter campus to a residential campus. Our headcount is about 13,300; full-time equivalency is just about 11,500.

Recently, I went to a conference in Michigan for museum directors and Bob Archibald, president of the Missouri Historical Society, talked about place and the importance of place in people's lives. My family has many generations personally invested in this place. My mother finished her bachelor's here. My dad got his master's here. Both of my sisters have degrees from here. My wife, my step-daughter, and my nephew graduated from here, and I received two degrees here.

I think it was in 1969 or 1970, when I had Bill Linden for a philosophy course in aesthetics and he took the whole class outside for a walk around the campus. He pointed out examples of the 10 principles of Zen aesthetics and how Gyo had incorporated those principles into the environment of the campus. Most people who walk through the campus wouldn't have an awareness of the principles or the design intention. Someone like Bill Linden, however, could see it within the context of his academic discipline. So, people were aware of Gyo's work. That is probably where I learned to see it as a garden.

Eric B. Barnett is the Director of The University Museum at Southern Illinois University Edwardsville.

RIGHT Students find the campus conducive to study and community

NEIMAN MARCUS

HOUSTON, TEXAS

GYO OBATA: DESIGNING A TREASURE HOUSE

I was working in my HOK office one Saturday afternoon when Stanley Marcus called from Houston. He told me that he purposely called on a Saturday afternoon because he wanted to find a team of architects who liked working hard.

Word of mouth brought me the Neiman Marcus commission. I had designed a house in St. Louis for John Wilson, the financial officer of Anheuser-Busch Companies. He asked Eleanor Le Maire, an interior designer, to do the interiors. She was a sensitive designer and colorist with a commanding presence.

When Stanley Marcus was thinking about building a store in Houston, Eleanor told him to interview me. This project marked the beginning of a major shopping mall, The Galleria in Houston. Neiman Marcus became the first entity of that mall. I advised Stanley that I always thought of Neiman Marcus as a treasure house, and would design one for him. He hired me.

We created the store in a very tight spot, and had to address its functional needs. I sketched many different schemes with all kinds of shapes on the outside. When I developed ideas, I grappled with different ways of solving problems. I hit on one special scheme. With Eleanor's help, we made the main floor much higher than in most department stores. At 25 feet high, it felt spacious, and just right for a treasure house.

Most retail stores avoid natural lighting. They want everyone's attention focused indoors, on shopping. I put onyx marble on the outside, which we lit from behind, so it would glow at night. During the day it would seem light, but at night the whole place would glow through the onyx and people could see the veins coming through. Stanley liked it.

Stanley was thoughtful, quiet, and dignified. I knew I was in the presence of a thinker. If I presented an idea he liked, he would say, "Let's go ahead and do it." Stanley wanted the space to be inviting when people entered his store. He asked for a beautiful area to walk through, with a sunken garden, evergreens, flowers, and shrubbery. I enjoyed having a client who gave me the freedom and responsibility to design.

LAWRENCE MARCUS: A BOLD EXPRESSION OF GOOD TASTE

It is a difficult job to create a new building, and this was a different kind of building.

When I got out of the army in 1946, I joined the company permanently. I was 29, and had already worked for the company since I was six years old. My first job was sticking pins in the pincushions for the leading fitter who worked especially for my Aunt Carrie. My father, his sister Carrie, and her husband, Al Neiman, started the company in 1907 and ran it by themselves until 1928, when my brother Stanley joined the company.

My father was a romanticist. An architecturally oriented person, he appreciated the beauty of Renaissance and European architecture, without being a serious student of architecture. He graduated high school and taught himself the culture of the old world, reading Plato, Aristotle, and Gibbons as a teenager. When he went to Europe in 1937, he wrote, "We have been looking around and what I like are the Giottos and the Brunelleschis and the things in the museums, but there is not much to report on fashion," which is interesting because fashion was his business.

In Europe he liked the museums and the architecture of the Renaissance period. I mention that because his interest influenced the building constructed in 1913, which was contemporary for those days, but incorporated many architectural refinements of the Renaissance period. He hired a local architect to build the first store, as the company had started out in rented quarters in 1907. That remained the only store until roughly 1950, when we built a suburban store.

By 1928, my brother Stanley had graduated from college and had taken his place in the company. He was beginning to influence the direction of the company and its style. In 1929, my Uncle Al and my Aunt Carrie divorced. That left my father, his sister, and my oldest brother in charge. My father was a leading idealist. He was a dreamer who happened to have some executive functions.

At that time, we were facing the need to expand. In 1934, when I was in high school, the family took a trip to Tulsa to see a shop that was available; we decided not to buy that. In other words, we were thinking of expansion, but did not get around to it. My father was prudent and could not picture how he could run a fashion store long distance. Finally we realized that if we didn't do it, other people would come and take our territory. We got busy and purchased property in the Houston suburbs.

LEFT High ceilings and generous spaces create an inviting place to shop

After making the purchase, a gentleman who had been in business there for many years said, "Look, fellows, I'd just as soon quit the business. Why don't you buy me out and you will have a going business." We agreed and bought it, not realizing what miserable shape it was in. We did some immediate repairs and spent more money than intended, refurbishing a building we did not plan to occupy very long. We had already bought the property on the outskirts.

Along came a young engineer named Gerald Hines who carried a slide rule in his pocket all the time and continually referred to it to answer almost any question he was asked. He was persuasive, yet made quite a deal with the help of the Neiman Marcus staff. We paid extremely low rent in order to be the leading store in the new development that Gerald Hines was working on: The Galleria. So we proceeded with our plans for the building while Gerald was still trying to line up clients to lease the rest of the property he was preparing to develop.

Obviously, Stanley respected Gyo because we had considered other extremely well-known architects in the country. We had engaged Eliel Saarinen and his son to design our suburban store in Dallas, which became part of the Northpark Center. And we were interviewing for the development of the Fort Worth store because the man who was the principal social and business leader in Fort Worth said, "If you guys don't build a store here, I am going to keep the ladies from coming over and shopping in Dallas." We had both the Galleria store in suburban Dallas and the suburban store in Fort Worth happening at the same time that we were working on the Houston store.

So Gyo, Gerald Hines, local architect Harwood Taylor, and I went on a tour of the country. We went out to the West Coast to see what was going on there. I remember being in the airport café waiting for our plane, and asking Gyo what he had in mind for this store. He took a paper napkin off the table and drew a little sketch of the building. When and how he got the idea, I do not have the slightest notion. But it satisfied the thing we were looking for, which was an expression of good taste, boldness, authority, dependability, and a pleasant, inviting place to shop. I would guess that was probably the only instruction that Gyo had.

As executive vice president, I was designated by my brother, father, and aunt to undertake the responsibilities for the Houston area. Miss Eleanor Le Maire was our interior designer. She had a strong personality and very definite points of view, so she became the designated hitter. We could not change a fixture or color without her approval. She had a theory of how colors would gently lead people from one department to another: the values would stay the same, but the hues would change. She had very positive points of view and a very strong influence. Nobody argued with Miss Le Maire. She surrounded herself with good people who were architecturally oriented and who followed her instructions well. Her influence is still there.

The building's exterior satisfies the qualities of our vision. What is not evident from the pictures is how dominant those tall, onyx windows on the second floor are. The onyx has a yellowish or golden look to it. The theory behind it was that in the daytime, the sun going through the onyx would cast a golden glow inside the building. At night time, the natural lights of the building would glow and make it look like a shrine. My only disappointment was that the daytime glow never materialized because we had to use the spaces behind the onyx for stock rooms.

One of the exciting parts of the project was saving the trees. There were three giant oak trees that must have been on the property for 50–100 years before we went there. We had to build boxes 12 feet in diameter around them and had to take down all the power and telephone wires in the neighborhood in order to move them. We broke one derrick and had to bring in a bigger one to take out the giant balls and big trees. We went a street over. We built boxes over boxes to keep the trees. A year and a half later, we had to go through the entire process again, to replant the trees. I think that at least one of those trees is still

alive. Gyo referred us to the landscape architect, Sasaki of Boston, who concurred on the idea of saving the trees.

Another exciting part involved the two sets of three flagpoles. We realized that the flagpoles had been set too close to the building and the flags were flapping against the structure and getting damaged. Gyo told us, "Move them somewhere else." We grouped the six flagpoles together and placed them overlooking the sunken garden. I was store manager at the time. I had made a set of 15 flags to show the history of the American flag, beginning with the Fleur-de-lis. During the American Bicentennial, I changed the flag story every month to show the progression of the American flag.

The building was designed to expand to another floor, but we determined it was too expensive to do it. After I left Houston, they did revamp the basement into all retail selling. I would say very definitely that our vision was accomplished with the aid of a fine building that exuded very fine quality. The building is elegant without being frivolous.

Lawrence Marcus is the retired Executive Vice President of Neiman Marcus.

RIGHT Panels of onyx glow at night and bathe the interior with light by day

UNIVERSITY OF MICHIGAN NORTHWOODS IV HOUSING

ANN ARBOR, MICHIGAN

GYO OBATA: ENVISIONING TOWNHOUSES FOR FAMILIES

HOK did something good for the students: we created a nice environment both inside and out for

graduate students and their families to live and study in, and enjoy.

All of the University of Michigan's buildings, housing, and other facilities were built out of steel and concrete and were very expensive. When the Board of Curators instructed the staff to hire a mass builder to put up single family houses for the students, the architects on the Board felt that would be a big mistake. They called me and asked if I could do the project and stay within the budget of a mass builder. I said that I would try, but first wanted to find a builder in Ann Arbor with an understanding of how to erect that type of structure.

We researched and came up with the right builder. After I conducted a rough study, I determined that instead of individual houses, townhouses would be a better, more efficient option, along with the creation of open spaces for families. Wanting to separate the traffic and cars from the families, I put in pockets and created an inner street

surrounded by buildings. I placed all the kitchens and dining on the inside, so parents could watch their children in the interior court while they were playing. We designed a series of courtyards to function as play areas; the parking was always away from the playground.

HOK conducted a study of the living habits of those student families. The students wanted a place to study quietly and needed a space to hang laundry. We gave each wood townhouse a full basement with laundry facilities, a main floor with a living room and dining room, and an upstairs with two or three bedrooms and small study alcoves. The students loved the buildings. The facilities people were very grateful to us because they did not have to use a mass builder. We solved that problem.

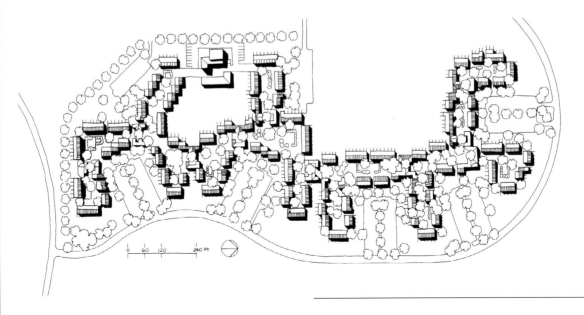

ABOVE The plan shows cluster courtyards and interior streets
LEFT Residents enjoy a sense of community and interaction

BOB CHANCE: MEANDERING STREETS AND COURTYARDS

I do know one thing that is unique about the project. It was the first and only project that I have ever seen with all of the section details drawn freehand, right to scale. The drawings were so carefully executed and well done that they were tremendously effective and innovative.

As assistant university architect, I was involved in selecting the architect. We went through a process at the university. First, the housing group determined they needed housing and got the funding together. Then it was a matter of choosing the architectural firm. We narrowed our options to 10 or 12, and then pared them down to four or six. We underwent a review process with the planning committee, which involved the user and the university architect's office, the university planner, and several others interested in the project.

We had a designated site, which helped determine what could happen there. Our program stated we wanted housing similar to a row housing concept. Gyo then came up with an idea that excited the group. He said, "I am envisioning a European street concept." That statement captured the committee members' imaginations and sold the project. It was a great concept and one of those very imaginative and fun designs.

I was familiar with Gyo and his office and a strong advocate for his firm to be interviewed. I met him at Cranbrook, where my sister was studying weaving and design, and Gyo was there studying with Saarinen. HOK had a strong, well-organized firm and a staff capable in all of their disciplines. They had enthusiasm and interest in the project. That impressed our planning committee. HOK just had a great background and broad range of well-designed projects. We knew if we chose them, they would end up doing a well-executed design and that it would be a successful project. Six to eight people were making the decision. Then it went to the university architect's office for selection. We happily recommended Gyo's firm.

Gyo expressed sincere interest in the project. He assured us he was going to give his very best. He was fantastically good at this. I had been involved with many architects

LEFT Safe playground areas are visible from kitchen windows

from all over the country and Gyo was right up there on top. If I were asked who were the five most impressive presenters, Gyo would be among them.

I recall a funny story that Gyo does not remember. We were at a meeting and had been working for hours. Gyo would just immerse himself in the process and nothing else mattered. He had a plane to catch and I was going to drive him to the airport from Ann Arbor up to Metro, a good half-hour trip. I suggested we wrap up so he could catch his plane, but he was so intensely involved in the project. After another 20 minutes I reminded him again that we needed to leave. He said, "I just have to talk about one more detail." More time passed and I was really concerned. I finally said, "Gyo, we have to go now or you will miss the plane." We ran and jumped in the car, raced well over the speed limit out toward the airport and I ran out of gas. I coasted over to the side. Gyo jumped out of the car, grabbed his attaché case, took a $20 bill out of his wallet and waved it while walking down the highway. Somebody stopped, picked him up, and he made the plane.

The exciting part of the project was that it was different from anything we had seen. The meandering European street was clever and inventive. It captured our imaginations and was an interesting and fine concept. It was accepted very well right from the beginning and still works well today. Northwoods IV was the first one, and when Northwoods V was to be done, there was no question that Obata would be the architect. The housing was well thought out. We were pleased and relieved that the architect performed so well. There were no problems of any consequence and the plans fell within budget. Gyo delivered the perfect solution and his design fulfilled all of our dreams and desires.

There were so many projects and great architects with whom we worked. As an architect, I was involved in many interesting projects, which gave me wonderful opportunities to compare the work and creative processes of others. It was a delight to work with Gyo and his people: Chester Roemer, Bob Edmonds, and Chip Reay. Professional, confident, and capable, they communicated sincere interest in their projects and the desire to give their best. The collaboration between client and architect was a great experience!

Bob Chance was the Assistant University Architect at the University of Michigan in Ann Arbor. He is retired.

FRED MAYER: A NEW, DENSE, EUROPEAN-STYLE VILLAGE

It has sort of a residential village quality like any number of little villages in Europe that have the peaked roofs and wood siding. The density has a European scale to it. Visually, it expresses the character of a small residential village, which is what it was meant to be.

I came to the University of Michigan on January 1, 1966. I drove up from Washington, D.C., on New Year's Day and listened to football games as I went. I came here as Assistant University Planner and held that position until mid-1968, when my boss moved on to a position at Columbia University in New York. I was made University Planner and served in that position until 2003. I had a wonderful time and we did an amazing number of projects in that period. I actually lived to see the concept for the campus fulfilled.

In those days, we started building what we called married-student housing, now called family housing. After World War II, the G.I. Bill exploded enrollments. We put people up in old war-time housing out at Rural Run Airport and other makeshift facilities and built our first family housing in 1948. But we did not have land

for appropriate housing for families with kids. When we acquired the North Campus in the early 1950s, we decided to build three projects: Northwoods I, II, and III. They were typical two-story, brick buildings with apartments above and below, a style found on most major universities.

By the late 1960s, our campus and town were short on space for our growing population of married students. We recognized a need to build more of this kind of housing and decided to build another phase of our Northwoods housing.

Our selection committee included university professional staff, administration representatives including the Vice President for Business and Finance to whom all university architects and planners reported, and some user groups like University Housing. The key individual was the University

ABOVE Parking outside the clusters allows for safe, social activity
RIGHT Mature trees enhance the sense of neighborhood

Architect, Howard Hackett. We narrowed a long list of qualified firms to between three and six, and scheduled interviews.

I am sure HOK made the list because of previous experience with Hellmuth, Yamasaki and Leinweber, a firm that worked on the earlier Northwoods units. HOK was gaining a national reputation for its quality design. They were selected and delivered a design that was a clear departure from traditional apartment configurations of above and below. They used a townhouse configuration that gave each family a vertical slice of the building, from the basement to the roof.

The other departure concerned site planning. Earlier apartments were sited in complexes where residents enjoyed pleasant grounds with mature trees, but had no central, focal space. This design introduced an interior courtyard, a common area that would serve as a pedestrian spine and also provide play areas, sandboxes for the little kids, and a hard surface on which older kids could ride their big wheels.

At the time, inflation was rampant in Michigan. We had several projects that came in way over the bids. Everybody feared this one would do the same. Since this was financed by the students' rent, the director of housing insisted on trying to keep the rent as low as possible. We used typical residential construction with two-by-fours and a wood exterior, when most of our buildings up to that point had been concrete block with brick exterior.

At the last minute, we took the site plan and cheapened it. The original plan, which won design awards, used quality paving materials in the courtyard. We put down asphalt and asphalt curbs to lower costs. Although the project came in under budget, we've had to repeatedly rebuild it, spending five or six times more than if we had done it to original specifications.

The interior court became the unifying element of the design. Someone from housing mentioned that the layout inspired people to relate to neighbors across the court, but they didn't talk to anyone else at Northwoods III. Curiously, in the plan, Gyo had shown a site for a community center, which we didn't have the money for right away. Eventually, we did build one, but we relocated it to a different site, and it's not accessed as much as it might have been.

The concept was definitely accomplished. The units have always been very popular and, in the early 1970s, we built Northwoods V, also designed by HOK. We added some bigger units because larger families were coming in. You do not often find universities building the same thing twice.

If you went out there today with the original rendering in your hand, you would recognize it. There would be no question that this was Northwoods IV. It is still there, still popular and still doing the job very well.

Fred Mayer was the University Planner at the University of Michigan in Ann Arbor. He retired in 2003.

GYO OBATA: JUMP-STARTING THE TREND TOWARD MIXED-USE CENTERS

Movement and light are design principles that play a major role in every project. Light floods the Houston Galleria through the skylight and calls attention to the fluid movement of people within the spacious retail center.

When developers build a mall, they usually have anchors at either end with shops in-between. Stanley Marcus talked with developer Gerald Hines, and asked him to interview me for the Galleria project. As it turned out, we were hired to work on the entire mall.

We wanted to design a very dense, compact shopping center—on three levels—to include department stores, shops, hotels, office buildings, and even a roof-top athletic club. We also wanted a special feature in the middle that would draw visitors to the shopping center. Using Rockefeller Center as our example, we developed the idea of putting in an ice rink. People commented, "An ice rink in Houston?" Running the length of the area was a skylight. Inspiration for the skylight came from Milan, Italy. The Galleria Vittorio Emanuele II, designed by Guiseppe Mangoni in 1861, has a skylight through the entire mall.

Gerald Hines took a chance on doing what we called a mixed-use center—the first one in the country—that combined shops and department stores with hotels and office buildings. The goal was to create a community of buildings by integrating different activities with shopping. Most vital communities around the world combine residential with shopping and workplaces. European cities are all essentially mixed-use environments. We strove to create that with the Houston Galleria.

During the planning phase, I paid particular attention to the movement and flow of people from Neiman Marcus to the center and from the center to the hotels and office buildings. Movement is a vital component in my design. Consequently, The Galleria became a meeting place for the people of Houston. And Neiman Marcus and the mall complement each other well.

This project jump-started the trend for shopping centers everywhere to become mixed-use centers. Subsequently, we designed many mixed-use centers and other developers followed that lead. Gerald Hines must have been pleased with our work because he then hired us to design the Dallas Galleria.

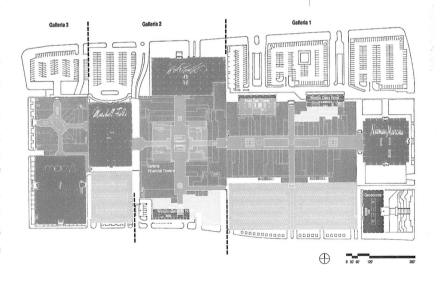

GERALD D. HINES: A BREATHTAKING PLACE FOR PEOPLE WATCHING

Houston Galleria was imaginative! It had fantastic interior space and significant amenities!
It was also a forerunner that urged others forward, so that today you have an interior
ski slope in centers in Madrid and Dubai.

I just love to develop, so I love to work with architects. I understand their initiatives and sometimes where they are going. But you have to understand where they are going because they may be taking you down the wrong path. You have to get on the same path. Houston Galleria was a pretty serious project for me. I had two major projects—this and One Shell Plaza going at the same time. They were extending my network way beyond what it should have been. Development is a creative and very dangerous business. Not many developers have lasted 50 years. They have gone broke. It is a very high-stakes game.

We were in the process of securing Neiman Marcus on our site and Stanley Marcus had an interiors person, Eleanor Le Maire, who recommended that Stanley talk to Gyo Obata about the store building. Stanley then said, "Gerry, why don't you talk to Gyo. Just see what you think because I think I'm going to have him design my building, my store."

We started to get involved with building The Galleria and it came time to choose an architect. I had never done any work with Gyo Obata. I asked two architects, Neuhaus and Taylor, who I had worked with and had done a number of small buildings for me, to design a concept of what they thought The Galleria should be. Then I asked Gyo Obata to do one. I liked Gyo's plan and concept much better.

Since I was not familiar with his project approach and philosophy, I was concerned that Gyo might be a "gold-nugget" architect, which meant that he would not listen to his client. As it turned out, Gyo was very flexible.

LEFT Offices and hotel overlook the shopping area
RIGHT Shopping, dining, and ice skating under the skylights

We came up with exteriors that were of pea gravel, exposed aggregate, or perhaps I should say, stone. It may not have been as good as what was put on Neiman Marcus, but it was a very compatible look.

Gyo had a scheme that featured a parking garage on Westheimer Road. That was extremely hard for me to swallow because Westheimer and Post Oak Boulevard were our presentation streets. So, we only went underground on the front, although conceptually, Gyo was right. Parking on both sides would have been more utilitarian, but I guess I was a little old-fashioned and felt that people should see the front. Because this was my first big retail complex, I went with my instincts, which probably were right. Later on we have seen Gyo's concepts throughout the world, which provide parking on both sides of the street.

Then, as we started to plan, I told Gyo I was worried about the basement and how we would energize that basement. He said, "Gerry, why not an ice-skating rink?" I said, "No one builds an ice-skating rink inside a mall. They all build them on the outside or adjacent and enclosed." Well, I looked at it and thought that it might not be a bad idea. We ran our numbers and we felt we could do it; we could build the spans that were necessary to cross the ice-skating rink and create a very interesting structure. So we proceeded on that.

Then Gyo came up with the idea that there ought to be an interior way of navigating the environment that feels instinctive. That is when he introduced the skylight that runs completely through the center, which made The Galleria similar to its namesake in Milan, except that it is bigger. With the brilliant addition of the skylight, people have no problem understanding where they are inside of our structure.

I have taken that lesson and we are using that concept in some of the things that we are doing in Milan today. I think that some of those basic principles were very good. My concern about the rentals in the basement were negated when we finally achieved a rental equal to what we had on the ground floor, the fashion floor.

People just love to watch people. That is what happened in The Galleria. It became a circulatory promenade. People walked to see other people. The width of that mall was very generous. It is a huge space and a common space with a skylight right down the middle. I thought it was too generous at the time, but I went with it. People told me I was crazy because people wanted to shop from one side across to the other and that could not be done in The Galleria. But it drew the crowds and we proved them wrong. It was very good because the traffic on weekends and evenings was tremendous. So, we earned a reputation for ourselves. I think that this project put us on the map.

Initially, The Galleria was a one-department-store mall. That was very difficult. Most malls have two major anchors. We eventually had three: Lord & Taylor, Saks, and Macy's. We then had the expansion of Galleria II, Galleria III, and Galleria IV to make it the largest retail complex in Houston. So, I think that working with Gyo, and his imagination and our willingness to put our pocketbooks where our heads were, worked out. We owned The Galleria for more than 30 years, so it was not a speculative project. It continued to grow in value and was recently expanded.

The Galleria is a really exciting space. People were amazed at the scope of the interior. It's not just a mall that is 30 feet wide. It has breadth, width, height, and volume that really create excitement. It was utterly breathtaking for the citizens of Houston and those who came down to see it. Witnessing that is the great part about the development business.

Gerald D. Hines is the founder and Chairman of Hines Interests, an international real estate firm.

ANTHONY'S RESTAURANT & BAR

ST. LOUIS, MISSOURI

GYO OBATA: CREATING DINING AMBIENCE

Lighting is the most important part of any restaurant. It sets the atmosphere, creates a sense of private space, provides visual enjoyment of the meal served, and enhances the overall dining experience.

Tony and Vince Bommarito first opened a storefront restaurant in St. Louis. My brother Kim, who had a studio on a boat on the river, used to go there to eat with me. Tony was the cook and Vince was the maître d'. They served good food in a space where the décor was traditional and functional, with tables covered in checkered oil cloth. When the brothers decided to open a second place, Anthony's Restaurant & Bar, on the first floor of the Equitable Building, Anthony's became one of my first restaurant projects.

The secret of restaurant design is the lighting. The dining space was rectangular in shape, so I installed glass walls and made a dark floor and a dark ceiling. Then I dropped a beautiful Alvar Aalto lamp over each table. The tables were draped in white linen tablecloths. The effect was such that when you sat for a meal, you felt as though you and your dining partners were the only group in the restaurant.

The bar is a square room, so I placed the seating around the bar. In the middle, I made a hanging design of all the glassware and illuminated it. As everyone sits around the bar, the glassware becomes the ornamental feature in the center. A few tables dot the perimeter. The room has high ceilings with glass on one side, a wood wall on one side, and windows, which can exacerbate noise levels. We quieted the space with sound-absorbent acoustical ceilings and carpeting. Tony has very good taste and is a real supporter of modern architecture and design.

Throughout the years, many changes occurred, but the bar remains true to its original design. Sometimes when a design is understated, simple, and minimal, its timeless appeal advocates its longevity. Anthony's is still considered one of the best in town.

LEFT Hanging, illuminated glassware serves as a focal point and sculpture
ABOVE Relaxed, quiet dining areas

41

ANTHONY M. BOMMARITO: A CONTEMPORARY DINING EXPERIENCE

We had a great opportunity to do something different in the city. Today our restaurant

design still looks great and is a focal point for that part of St. Louis.

I am the owner of A. Bommarito Wines. We distribute wine from all over the world in the state of Missouri. It's an exciting job and I have been very blessed. I took this career turn about 16 years ago and it has been a rewarding venture.

At the time of the project with Gyo and HOK, my brother Vince and I were operating Tony's Restaurant. There was a new building, the Equitable Building, going up at the other end of downtown. It was probably the first new construction downtown in some time. Ray Wittcoff was the developer and Gyo was the architect on the project.

I met Gyo when he first came to St. Louis. He would come to the restaurant, where my brother and I were in business together, and order a little plate of spaghetti. My brother Vince and I were just young kids and did not know much about architects or their work. We visited with Gyo and saw the Abbey and some of his projects around the country. Gyo was always very friendly and personable. When we learned he was doing a new building and the opportunity came along for us to be a part of it, the idea of working with him intrigued us.

The developers of the Equitable Building were interested in putting a restaurant on the first floor. They came to us and talked about the project. At that time, the conversations went back and forth as to whether or not we should do another downtown restaurant. We already had one just a few blocks away—a traditional Italian restaurant with

LEFT Alvar Aalto lighting creates a warm, intimate environment

candles and red-checkered cloths. The new building offered a complete departure from that conventional environment because Gyo obviously was on the contemporary end of things. This caught our interest. Knowing that our restaurants' atmospheres would be separate and distinct assured us that our businesses would not compete with one another.

In 1968, I had worked in New York at the 21 Club. Two restaurants caught my eye: one was the Four Seasons, which was on the contemporary side; the other was the Ground Floor in the CBS Building, another contemporary restaurant. I had seen these two exciting restaurants open in New York. They were completely different from any in St. Louis. And I said, "That concept would fit right into that building."

It was a great benefit to deal with a worldly person like Gyo. We could mention the places we'd seen and watch his eyes open up in recognition and understanding. He had an immediate sense of what it was we were trying to accomplish. When we held conversations about what we wanted. Gyo knew and understood. From the very beginning, I felt that we were on the same page as far as design and atmosphere. In those discussions, I told him that I have always been sensitive and aware of my restaurant customers and noticed that they feel warm, comfortable, secure, and protected when their table is near a wall. I did not like booths. I wanted all tables and I wanted it to be private. The other restaurant floor plan had people sitting next to each other. I wanted this space to be more intimate.

At the time, Gyo had to shift his focus to his growing firm, so he passed our project to other members of HOK; but he always had his finger on it. Based on discussions we had with Gyo, HOK presented different designs. For example, I remember Gyo drawing a line on paper and saying, "Put a glass wall here." It was brilliant. The large room was divided by glass partitions with a bronze tint. A reflection came off the glass and bounced through the dining room, which made it interesting. Also, every table was by some stationary object, whether it was a wall or a glass partition. The room was segmented, and not just a cold, open space like other restaurants. Some tables at the front of the restaurant looked onto the beautiful lobby garden of exotic trees and plants. Every table felt special and intimate, which excited me.

We talked about the lighting and wanted to make sure it was not too bright. Gyo came up with the idea of bringing the lights down and hanging them over the tables. That's a common motif now, but you did not see that in 1972. There were not many lights in the whole dining room; it was a dark room with a light over each table. When we talked about these things, I liked the idea, but could not begin to envision the results. I just trusted that Gyo would make it great.

We separated the dining room from the bar so that if the bar was busy and noisy, that would not filter into the dining room. The two rooms operated independently, but still had continuity. They both felt and looked the same. And the bar is still intact today. It is still simple, tasteful, and mostly true to the original design.

In bar design, it is known that people do not like to sit and stare at other people. So HOK designed a centerpiece behind the bar, inspired by a piece of Charles O. Perry artwork in the lobby courtyard. On the walls, we had only four pieces of art which were lit up and designed in such a way that they looked like they were coming out of the wall. You could look at the dark room and then look over and see color popping out of the wall. It was unique and peaceful.

ANTHONY'S RESTAURANT & BAR

The same lights hanging over the tables were hanging from about a 28-foot ceiling over the bar. I think Gyo had seen the lights in Finland. I don't know if everyone appreciated how well the lobby, dining room, and bar tied together visually, but I know the input from Gyo and HOK put everything in relationship.

HOK told us to use warm tones. We carpeted the floor and walls with brown carpet. When I told people, "We are carpeting the walls," they thought I was a little nuts. But it was meant for acoustics, so that the room was a very quiet, soft, elegant, and contemporary dining room. Today, restaurant design is almost the opposite. People don't want quiet; they want noise. I think if there was a difficult sell for some people, it was that the room was too quiet, too soft. But if you wanted to be out for a special night or needed quiet to talk business, this was the perfect place.

When we opened the restaurant, only a couple of details needed to be refined. As people sat at the tables and looked up, they could see the bottom of the light bulbs. I told Gyo about that and we agreed that we needed to lower them a couple of inches so that people would focus on their table partner and not on the lights.

The project was quite an experience. I found it exciting from both a design and an operational point of view. From the dining room to the kitchen, it all worked well. Everything flowed. I wanted for nothing, not even an additional electrical outlet.

Anthony's was a complete change from the style of food we served. Only eight blocks away, we served Italian food. This was more contemporary culinary fare, maybe with a little French overtone. People sometimes thought of it as a French restaurant, but that was never the intention. Those who knew me as someone always in the kitchen cooking Italian food thought I had suddenly changed. It took me a while to adjust to that.

People would come in saying they wanted pasta and I would say, "Sorry, but no. You can order that in the restaurant down the street." That was hard for me because I was always brought up taking care of people, giving them what they wanted. And we did not want our restaurants to compete with one another. We had created two separate restaurants and it was difficult for people to see what we were trying to do. Even the hours were different. One was open for lunch; the other was not. We had to educate our customers about Anthony's softer and different style of service .

When you are young, it is good to change things and easier to adjust. Some of the changes, and the building in which they took shape, continue to this day. Anthony's is still a tasteful, elegant space.

This was a great little project, not only for Vince and me personally, but also for HOK. We all benefited from the publicity it generated. A lot of thought went into making Anthony's what it is. It is not just another restaurant, but a warm, intimate, St. Louis landmark dining experience.

During the project, Anthony and his brother Vince Bommarito operated Tony's Restaurant. Anthony is now the owner of A. Bommarito Wines in St. Louis, Missouri.

RIGHT Natural, filtered light illuminates the tasteful, elegant space

GYO OBATA: A PLACE FOR THE COUNTRY'S BEST MINDS

There have been many books written about the history of the computer industry and Silicon Valley; this is the site where the personal computer was invented. In architecture, all buildings need to be wedded to their sites. Here, landscape and light inform the design, the way the building steps down the hillside and opens to the light.

George Pake, now deceased, was a friend of mine from Washington University, where he was the Provost. From St. Louis, he moved to Palo Alto, California, to serve as the first director of the Palo Alto Research Center, then a wholly owned subsidiary of the Xerox Corporation. He asked me to design the center and invited me to California to look at a building site. PARC was to be an interdisciplinary hub that Pake hoped would attract the most imaginative and intelligent scientists and inventors.

When I saw the Coyote Hill Road property, I told Pake that we should build a very low, one-story structure on the first floor and let the building fall down the hillside, so that neighboring residents who wanted to preserve the integrity of their community would only see a low profile of the research center. The residents approved.

A physicist and educator, Pake eagerly anticipated bringing scientists together. He asked for a small, 10- by 12-foot office for each of the scientists, with labs and meeting areas nearby. He insisted on daylight in all of the offices. HOK's challenge was to design a building cascading down a hillside in a way that would capture maximum natural light. The site became a fundamental design issue.

We created courtyards that flooded offices with light. The labs were inside and did not need natural light. We grouped them in a series of clusters. The structure was composed of concrete and glass. From the outside, the building is almost non-descript; from the inside, it is quite bright and beautiful.

On this site, Xerox research came up with the first individual computer. At the time, Xerox was more interested in copy machines; however, Steve Jobs knew what happened at that lab. He started Apple and that company took off. What George Pake did was extraordinary. Xerox asked him to find new products and inventions, so he built this building, and he brought together the best minds in the country.

UNCOVERING PERSPECTIVE ON PARC

One summer day in 2008, six people gathered at a round table in the Information Center at Palo Alto Research Center for a discussion of PARC and its building's history. The original project client, George Pake, passed away in March 2004.

Around the table with Marlene Birkman sat Kathy Jarvis (above, right), manager of the Information Center, Dana Bloomberg, Vice President of Operations, Sonal Chokshi, a writer, Daniel Swinehart (middle), Manager of Intellectual Property Creation, and David Biegelsen (left), Research Fellow, Electronic Materials Lab, engineer and inventor.

Reflecting on George Pake, Biegelsen described him as a wonderful, ethical person, a Midwesterner, and someone interested in St. Louis culture and architecture. Biegelsen was a graduate student at Washington University in St. Louis, where George Pake served as Provost. In March 1970, Pake offered Biegelsen a job at the Palo Alto Research Center before the building was constructed.

Biegelsen described the early working environment: "We were squatting in rented quarters on Porter Drive. It was a little building with two atria and we were really crammed in there. We then expanded into a building across from here with leased quarters, and even moved into a third building. We always felt quite dispersed and as if we were living within the bounds. When money became available from Xerox to construct a building, we were quite excited about it. Everybody wanted to provide input about its design and amenities, saying, 'We want this and we want that.' Of course, the Green Foothills Committee put all kinds of restraints on our ability to use this land, which delayed this building for well over a year or two."

One of things that Xerox had to do to get its 99-year lease on the site was to lease the site adjacent to it and only board horses there. Pake was the first person to have a successful breakthrough with the Green Foothills Committee (formed in the early 1970s). He got them to approve construction of the building. Another reason for the nod was that Gyo Obata and HOK would design the building to fit into the environment. The original drawings showed levels that fit in the hillside with trailing plants, creating a building integrating lush greenery. According to Biegelsen, "It looked like the Hanging Gardens of Babylon."

The hot issue, according to Swinehart, was preserving the environment and engineering the building around the existing trees. He elaborated, "There is an oak tree here and that is why the building goes one way and back around the other." Also, the color of the concrete used in the exterior

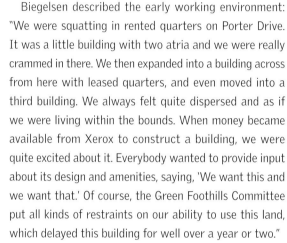

LEFT Greenery is integrated with the architecture
RIGHT Courtyards separate the pods and provide accessible greenspaces

walls had to match the color of the hill, and extension berms were built along the road to keep the site from looking industrial. The area was part of the Stanford Industrial Park and Highway 280, which won awards for its beauty.

The San Andreas Fault posed a natural constraint. Biegelsen described how the seismically active area helped inform the design: "The key design element is that the building is built on slabs and each of the pods is relatively independent. When we had the 1989 earthquake, the building survived. It had a million-dollars worth of damage. Where the different pods came together, they were bridged by metal joints that allowed the buildings to move relative to each other. It was a surprising polarization of the ground movement that had not really been planned on in the design. What is amazing is that the building survived."

Swinehart recalled the loss of cinderblock around the elevators due to the quake. There were some dangers, but nothing structural, although the building manager believed another 14 or 20 seconds of acceleration might have shaken concrete off the pillars. Reflecting on the design integrity, Swinehart noted that above the first floor, the main support along that part of the building could break in two, so that the part built under the hill could vibrate independently of all the other pods.

Biegelsen reflected on the lab operations and PARC culture. "PARC has a company structure that mirrors its pod design," he said. "There are centers of excellence, different areas of expertise, that all come together, but not in a standard way. PARC has always nurtured this tension because it is facilitative."

"The architecture," continued Biegelsen, "lends itself to having laboratories localized around an atrium. And then you have the tension about how to cross the boundary between this pod and that pod, between laboratories. There have been good studies that show how some people do this well, and others are destroyed at the prospect."

The building, according to Biegelsen, is laid out beautifully. "It seemed like the prime constraint was that everybody's office should have a window to the outside. That means a lot of surface-to-volume ratio. The clever way to accomplish that was to have these atria. But because of the oaks and the topography of the hills, the atria move along the hill. Everything isn't all lined up, which is pleasant when walking around." Until the new addition, the downside of that design was that people could not see more than 30 feet. It was difficult to gauge if people were in the building, or if they had gone.

Bloomberg elaborated, "Building in pods, with everyone having an office, is precious to people. People love their office space, and it assists in employee retention. In new buildings, that doesn't happen too frequently. Most people simply have 'cube space.'" Bloomberg reflected that having "everyone in an office is not the best for employee interaction, but at least the design of open areas on a couple of floors encourages group meetings and informal conversations."

"With the sight line," added Jarvis, "you don't see people. Everyone has an office and the maze-like quality of the pod makes it a quiet building. It is contemplative, and conducive to contemplative activity."

Given the necessary design constraints, the labs were expensive to design. Biegelsen explained that as experimentalists, they had to design their own labs and no lab was on top of another. They could not have easily installed chases to run all the infrastructure elements up and down. The building's concrete pads made it hard to dig into the floor.

Swinehart described how the building's original design did not foresee changes in technology: "When the building was constructed, the concept of a personal computer wasn't very strong. We had the classic time-sharing machine and mainframe; we had to be able to use them from our offices and we had to be able to distribute the communications using those terminals. We also had a network that required a concentration of machines in one room and some very elaborate wiring to the offices."

"One of the laboratories," Swinehart continued, "thought aggressively and industrially about the design. They put in a major machine room with steel doors, glass windows, and its own air conditioning system. Upstairs, there was a raised floor for running cables to offices with the awareness that individuals would probably be rewiring things themselves."

Swinehart explained that to this day, one section of the building has a raised floor, although it may have nothing to do with communications any more, but rather temperature controls. Elaborate wiring with coaxial cables eventually became totally obsolete. It had nothing to do with Ethernet, but with keyboard cabling, point to point. "The group planning that project," said Swinehart, "didn't think very hard about the heating and air conditioning and environment of those machines. They put them into a room that immediately overheated and it took a lot of experimenting with innovative cooling solutions to eventually get that under control. When Ethernet came along, we had to come up with imaginative ways for stringing those cables around."

"The building's exterior," according to Jarvis, "goes virtually unnoticed, which was an original design goal.

I don't think about how the building looks from the outside when you approach the building. I always tell people that they won't believe how big this building is inside. When you view the exterior in relation to the larger world outside, you don't really experience the building. You can't believe that this is a 200,000-square-foot building."

Chokshi closed the discussion with a contemplative thought about the building. She reflected, "My parents have been in Silicon Valley for more than 30 years. When they came here with me, they said it was like an ashram in Hindu culture. It felt like a place of seclusion, but at the same time, there was the distant awareness of being in the midst of many. The building seems like one of the metaphors that we have for our process and what happens around here."

Dana Bloomberg, Vice President of Operations, Katherine S. Jarvis, Manager of the Information Center, Sonai Chokshi, Writer and Content Specialist, Daniel C. Swinehart, Manager of Intellectual Property Creation, and David Biegelsen, Research Fellow, Electronic Materials Lab participated in a group conversation at Palo Alto Research Center.

GYO OBATA: DESIGNING BIG SPACES WITH GOOD CIRCULATION

This project began in 1966 and was a major commission on the National Mall in Washington, D.C. I was told it would attract many visitors because of America's love of aviation. The big idea in the design was the movement of people and the use of northern daylight to orient visitors as they circulate through the huge museum.

Washington, D.C., has a complicated construction approval process. We needed to obtain approvals from the National Capitol Planning Commission, the National Fine Arts Commission, and the Smithsonian Institution Executive Committee. But because of the Vietnam War, the project was cancelled. We were told that the museum would not be built until further funding could be procured.

Five years later, we were re-interviewed and rehired. The National Air and Space Museum got $40 million for the program, which had a whole new set of design specifications. The board membership also had changed, and astronaut Mike Collins was the museum director.

We designed a new scheme to coincide with the 1976 Bicentennial. The project requirements included designing auditoriums and places to display airplanes. Because many people would visit the museum, I had to think in terms of big spaces and good circulation flow. The idea of a mall came to me. I designed it on two levels, so that people coming in from the Washington Mall on Independence Avenue could walk along the Mall, visit the exhibits, and see Orville Wright's plane and John Glenn's capsule hanging in the large, open gallery.

The building faces north and south. On the south is Independence Avenue with heavy traffic and lots of sun, which we muted. We created a series of theatres with blocked-out areas for the aircraft displays. The Mall side faces north. There, I used big areas of glass because I did not have to worry about the sun's intensity. At night, people can look into the building and see all the airplanes.

As many as 50,000 people visit the National Air and Space Museum daily. During the summer tourist season, it is the most visited museum in the world. Wisconsin Senator William Proxmire, who used to issue the Golden Fleece Award for needless government spending, gave us a Reverse Award because up to that time, we were the only federal project that came in on time and on budget.

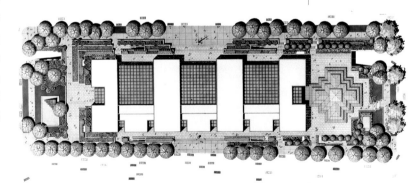

LEFT Large atria glow at night from illuminated airplanes and spacecraft

MIKE COLLINS: A GIGANTIC BUILDING FOR GIGANTIC OBJECTS

For a long time, this idea of a new museum in Washington on the Mall was just an idea. But when they dug that gigantic hole, I said to myself, "My God, this is really going to happen." While I don't want to belittle the beautiful building that rose up out of the hole, I must maintain that my most vivid memory is of a gigantic hole.

We had a site on Washington's National Mall before Gyo came along. It was not our own building, but a building called the Arts and Industries Building. It was crowded and antiquated. I did not select HOK to be the architect of the Air and Space Museum. Rather, I inherited Gyo. When I met him, I was delighted because I found him to be a wonderful person.

The Smithsonian Institution was the client. My boss, Dillon Ripley, was the Secretary of the Smithsonian, but he stayed out of the business of the Air and Space Museum and had little to do with the construction. For all intents and purposes, I was the client and Gyo was the architect.

There were a lot of different groups in Washington: the National Capitol Planning Commission, the Fine Arts Commission, and the Congress of the United States. The Congress appropriated the money and the money went to the Air and Space Museum. But in order to get the hole in the ground, we needed the permission of the National Capitol Planning Commission and the Fine Arts Commission. The National Capitol Planning Commission was a practical organization concerned with the usual routine—setback, power lines, and all the stuff that a city imposes on a builder. There were a lot of rules as to what we could and could not do, and they had to approve the plans from a practical point of view. Aesthetics and appearances were the bailiwick of the Fine Arts Commission which, as the name implies, was concerned with how the project looked and how it related to the surrounding buildings.

Looking at the project from Gyo's perspective in St. Louis, he might very well have looked out toward Washington and seen four behemoths: the Smithsonian; the Gilbane Building Company, the Air and Space Museum's project manager and agent for overseeing the work; the National Capitol Planning Commission; and the Fine Arts Commission. Gyo did not have to worry about the money because when he came on board, it had already been appropriated. I had to worry about the money.

LEFT The museum welcomes millions of visitors yearly

The Air and Space Museum possesses a giant collection of airplanes, spacecraft, and smaller memorabilia of one kind or another. Any building we constructed on the Mall in downtown Washington would only be able to exhibit a tiny portion of the vast collection. The pressure was on me to display Lindbergh airplanes, the Wright brothers' plane, and others. We needed a gigantic building, which I knew we could not put on that site. The problem I presented to the architect was to build as enormous a building as possible because 90 percent of our total collection would never make it into the building.

I started with a vacant lot and I spent a lot of time with Gyo trying to explain our collection to him, and what we hoped to achieve. He spent a lot of time rearranging the furniture in my living room. I'm a very conventional thinker, very orthogonal. My couch faced the fireplace and it was parallel to the rear wall. Gyo thought it ought to be 37 degrees from the front door and he had all the chairs arranged accordingly. I don't know if it was Feng Shui, but he completely rearranged my furniture. I remember thinking, "Well, I don't know. I am not sure I want everything 37 degrees out there on the Mall. That's going to look a little bit peculiar." But he did a wonderful job.

The Fine Arts Commission rejected the first design that Gyo put forth. He and I presented it together. The Chairman of the Commission, J. Carter Brown, was also the Director of the National Gallery of Art and came from a very wealthy Rhode Island family. We got through our

LEFT Marble cubes break up the building's mass facing the National Mall

presentation and Carter said he did not like it, stating, "It sits turgidly on its site." Well, what could we say to that? The rejection of this first design brought out what I think is one of Gyo's good qualities.

Granted, having a building on the Mall in Washington designed by HOK was undeniably a great feather in Gyo's cap. Any other architect could have thrown a snit at this stage of the game, but Gyo showed a great deal of flexibility. He returned to the drawing board and re-envisioned the building and how it was situated on the site. Gyo, along with Chih-Chen Jen, his right-hand man for design flourishes, and Jerry Sincoff, who assisted with

practical aspects, came up with a new building. The second building design also got rejected, but was judged as being closer. The third design Gyo presented to J. Carter Brown and the Fine Arts Commission was finally accepted. The bureaucracy in Washington gets criticized frequently; however, in this particular case, I think the Fine Arts Commission was right. The building that eventually rose up on the Mall was graceful and fit its location beautifully. It is as much a bureaucratic triumph as it is a tribute to Gyo's flexibility and perseverance.

The building, oddly enough, was pretty straightforward. The overriding thing was that we had gigantic objects, and, therefore, we needed gigantic interior spaces. It works. The flow patterns work very well. The entrance and the exits are mid-ship. People come into the central part of the building, immediately branch out and head for the ends of the building. Once they've seen those, they work back toward the central exits. It's an extremely efficient flow pattern, although I'm sure it's not the kind of flow pattern they would teach in architecture school.

Inside the building we planned to have a large, full-size planetarium that was yet to be donated to us by the West German government. I had to tell the architect exactly what was involved in building to accommodate it. So we hired a consultant to help troubleshoot what might be required in terms of interior space, electrical loads, floor loads, and ceiling heights. Trying to accommodate something that didn't yet exist was probably the most difficult part of the project.

I guess I knew enough about big projects and the National Aeronautics and Space Administration to know that something is always going to go wrong. NASA used to call it "the long pole in the tent"—that which held everything up. I spent most of my time worrying about what was going to go wrong and what was amazing was that so little did go wrong. I give a lot of credit to Gyo and HOK. They were flexible and responsive. And, I give a lot of credit to Gilbane Building Company. They were pros. They stayed on top of the contractors. I also credit myself and my staff for stating what we needed and not deviating or killing the project with changes.

Gyo, Jerry Sincoff, Chih-Chen Jen, and all the people involved were extremely easy to work with. We didn't throw snits or have big arguments. If we had a problem, we worked it out to our mutual satisfaction. It was a pleasant experience working with Gyo and HOK. Everything flowed smoothly.

The machinery of aviation and space does not ipso facto live harmoniously with other collections that make their home on the Mall such as works of art, Indian artifacts, and old dinosaur bones. So it is not the easiest thing in the world for an architect to house these machines and to do it in a way that says, "Okay, this building is a little different, but it's graceful and it seems to fit." Gyo's building projects a calm and peaceful image. It looks like it belongs. It's appropriate.

Michael Collins, Apollo 11 astronaut, is a former Director of the National Air and Space Museum. He is retired.

They did not want the building to be visible. They wanted the main space underground.

Roger Boas, a very bright guy, and the Chief Administrative Officer under Mayor Moscone of San Francisco, was responsible for getting this convention center completed. The site occupied an 11.5-acre redevelopment area. HOK competed with Skidmore, Owings and Merrill, who already had an established practice in San Francisco. We were essentially newcomers, but Roger chose us to do the project. Because we were the underdogs, I felt a strong responsibility to bring this project to fruition.

It was really a tough project because the people of San Francisco did not want a big convention center built. They wanted it to be the least visible, so we had to put it underground. Here we had a huge convention space, 640,000 square feet, a really large building for meetings,

exhibits, and events, that had to be buried. T.Y. Lin of San Francisco was the structural engineer, and a very good one. They developed a concrete structural system of inverted barrel arches to meet the requirements for underground construction. The arches were anchored to foundation beams.

What we did was create an entry building. From there, people took escalators down to the exhibit space. I wanted an arch, so the top of the structure is all covered. Since that time, I think that they have built over that.

There were a lot of roadblocks along the way: how to put it underground, and once it went underground, how to pay for the expense. Fortunately, Roger Boas was a very determined individual and we got the project built.

Moscone Center

ROGER BOAS: MEETING A CHALLENGE WITH TRIUMPH

Gyo was building his firm's base, so he was all over the place. But he always gave me whatever time I felt that I needed and was necessary.

In 1977, I took office as the city's Chief Administrative Officer. I was nominated by the then mayor, George Moscone, and received supporting votes by the Board of Supervisors. I had been a former supervisor myself and had left the government. George Moscone asked me to come back. I decided to try it for six months. I stayed for 10 years.

The year before I had come back, Moscone had put a proposal on the ballot to build a convention center. The only way he could get approval was to agree to build it underground. There were environmentalists with political clout pushing for an underground facility. The vote came through favorably in 1976. So in 1977, the first thing the mayor asked me to do was build the convention center (it wasn't named Moscone until after he was assassinated).

There were many distinguished architects from the city who wanted the job. HOK, who I had never heard of, also put in a bid. The architects all made very carefully prepared presentations, held in my office. I was the sole decision-maker, but I put together a team to give me their opinions. The HOK presentation was 100 percent Gyo Obata, and no one else said a word. I was favorably impressed and chose Gyo.

San Francisco is very contentious, with constant litigation. It is a hard city to govern, run by a bad charter put into effect after the fire and earthquake in 1906. My responsibilities and powers as Chief Administrative Officer were specified in the charter. Within the guidelines, I could do as I wished. No one, not even the mayor or the board, could stop me. So decision-making was easy.

I knew that the existing Civic Center was very small and inaccessible. We were losing business. I talked to the Convention Bureau and the hotel people, and they told me of their extraordinary need to have a place that could attract 25,000 to 35,000 people to the city at a crack.

As a young supervisor and member of the Board of Supervisors in 1963, I had tried to get a convention center built in the South of Market Area (SOMA), where Moscone is. On the map, it is the big north/south divide in San Francisco. The area was big, but dead. In the past, San Francisco was a manufacturing city: mattresses, telephone books, pencils, and ladies dresses were made there. Later, the area was composed of garages and parking lots. It was an absolute desert and a terrible financial liability to San Francisco. So, when we picked this land for Moscone,

it was land that belonged to the Regional Redevelopment Agency. It turned out to be the spark plug.

My first move toward building the center was finding a law firm that could win our battle. I interviewed 10 of the biggest law firms I could find that would understand this issue. I chose the right firm with the right litigator to head the team. They were expensive and cost us about $2 million. A feud came about that attempted to stop our plan. We fought in the courts and barely won. We earned the right to go ahead and it turned out to be an excellent investment.

It was a maniacal idea to build a convention center underground. Not one existed in the world and to do it in San Francisco, which sits on aquifers with ocean water just underneath, seemed insane. But that was the only way people would have it. We received a go-ahead and needed to build something.

I determined the square footage from calculations from the Convention and Visitors Bureau. I said, "We need this much exhibit space, this much meeting room space, and a big exhibition hall." Our exhibition hall could be totally underground, but I wondered what we would do on top. I then turned to a philosophical designer named Charles Eames, known for the Eames chair, among other things. He had an office in Santa Monica, so I went down to see him and inquire about what we should do on the top side of the underground convention center.

Eames directed me to someone in New Mexico who had built a craft museum with objects from all over the world. He thought one idea would be to put a craft center on top of the Moscone. So I worked with them and with HOK.

When I saw the initial HOK plans, I talked to them about it. I did not like it. I called Gyo in St. Louis and he flew out the next day. Gyo is extremely intelligent. He thinks carefully before he speaks and speaks in a mild fashion.

He is a marvelous facilitator of that sort of problem. The issue got straightened out.

I was the first person in city history to use a headhunter firm. I chose Heidrich & Struggles. They located a project manager who reported to me twice a day and who met constantly with Bill Valentine, Patrick MacLeamy, and their HOK colleagues. Contractors who really wanted the job themselves recommended the construction manager, Turner Construction from back east. They were great.

Everything came together. If problems arose in the design phase, HOK would bring their staff up to my office or I would go down to their office in San Francisco. Everything went smoothly and was always synchronized. Gyo Obata, Patrick MacLeamy, and Bill Valentine worked together seamlessly, with Gyo providing the inspiration, Patrick the management, and Bill the design. I enjoyed every minute of it.

When the design was finished, I had a nice model by Gyo and Bill on display in City Hall for people to view. I then went to the Board of Supervisors for approval. There were 11 Board members and I needed six votes. I could not get it to approval; only five voted for it and the rest wanted to turn it down.

I began lobbying the dissonant supervisors and they all rejected it until I came to Supervisor Dan White, a former police officer and fireman. I took White to the model,

a part-time secretary. One day, I got a call saying that the convention center was flooding and that half of the thousand or more chairs we had purchased were missing and had been stolen. I had not been in England five weeks before getting that call.

The engineers had told me they were concerned about the water. An underground, saltwater river from the ocean flows all around the building. They felt the best protection would be oyster shells. We put in millions of oyster shells to protect it from leaks, but somehow water got in. We had pumps running 24/7, but they were not pumping it out right. The headlines in the paper read, "CAO Boas said they would be leak-proof.'" I cut short my visit to Oxford and returned to deal with the problem. That was the only part we had not anticipated. We braced for panic, earthquake shakes, even a gunman or an assassin, but not a water leak.

My greatest pleasure came from working with a terrific triumvirate: Obata, MacLeamy, and Valentine. They were new to the city, were innovative thinkers, and were extremely responsive to me. I found Gyo to be extremely interesting and fun to be with. I became an admirer of his father's art. So my entire relationship with Moscone was worthwhile and to see the convention center finally become a reality and a success gave me great personal satisfaction.

At the time of the project, Roger Boas was San Francisco's Chief Administrative Officer under Mayor George Moscone. He is retired and writing a book on World War II.

showed it to him and told him what I had gone through, how I had been thinking about it, why the design was solid and sound, and what it would mean to the city. He gave me my sixth vote. A couple of months later, he shot both Mayor George Moscone and Supervisor Harvey Milk.

George's death shocked me. I also knew Harvey Milk. My wife and I would see him at the opera, downstairs at the bar. I liked him very much. To see both men die on the same day in the same horrible fashion was awful. I got a call from an advisor who suggested I name the convention center after George. And so I did.

When the Moscone Convention Center opened in 1981, I was invited to Oxford University as a Visiting Fellow, so off I went with my wife. They gave me an office and even

GYO OBATA: A TERRACED COMPLEX ON A HILLSIDE

We were just starting our San Francisco office, our first major office outside St. Louis. The reason we went to the "City by the Bay" was because Stanford University said that if we opened an office in San Francisco, they would let us design their graduate library. This project was a result of our western expansion.

At one time, Levi Strauss had a loft-style building in San Francisco for its executives and workers. The Haas family and other descendents of Levi Strauss decided to move the company closer in to a 28-story, high-rise building in Embarcadero Center. But with all the employees on the lower levels and the executives on the top levels, they lost their original family style environment. They consulted with developer Gerson Bakar and asked him to build a building that would bring the whole Levi family together.

Gerson conducted interviews, and although HOK was a candidate, San Francisco firm Arthur Gensler & Associates was initially favored. When Gerson called and told me, I suggested, "Why don't you first hold a design competition?" He liked the idea and as a result, we were chosen to design the buildings and Gensler was chosen to design the interiors.

The site below Telegraph Hill and Coit Tower consisted of four blocks. On Telegraph Hill, there are hillside homes leading up to Coit Tower. People living there are very concerned about development. San Francisco is a tough place to get anything approved.

Working out of our San Francisco office, we came up with a building and created a park. We designed a low-lined, seven-story structure that we terraced down the cascading hillside. We stepped back the building as it rose. That is why we have all these little balconies. Because of the location, the use of brick had to be a facing material to precast concrete. In the middle of the building is a big glass

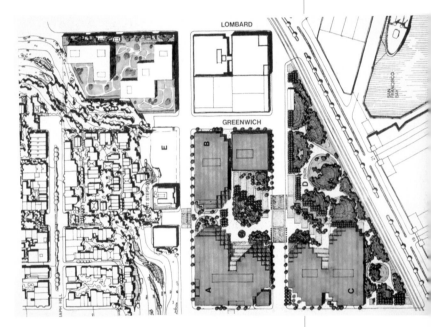

atrium with offices around it, where everybody who works there can come together. On the ground level we placed a restaurant, flower shop, and activities for people on the street. Landscape architect Lawrence Halprin created a beautiful park with a big fountain.

On April 8, 1982, Levi's Plaza was dedicated to the company employees. It is a fitting home for an enduring company. The core values of the company—empathy, originality, integrity, and courage—are inscribed on the entrance area of this unique place, nestled in the heart of San Francisco's Embarcadero.

LEFT Setbacks and balconies fit the scale of the hillside and neighborhood

GERSON BAKAR: A GIFT TO THE CITY

I am a developer. The Levi project is one of a kind and I am very proud of it, like any parent is of a child.

But as a developer, I hope to have that pride in all of my projects.

For years, Levi Strauss operated in a building on 98 Battery Street. As an employer, they were patriarchal. The key people in Levi, the Haas family, saw their employees on a regular basis because of the way the building was configured. They then moved into the Embarcadero Center and became the tenant in what is now Embarcadero Two, and was then known as the Levi Strauss Building.

Just like in many high-rise buildings, the executives and employees took different elevators. The employees were housed on the first 10 floors and the executives were on the upper floors. There were no lobbies in those buildings; people came off the public area and went up. There was no place where the mass of employees could see the executives.

I was a close friend of Mr. Walter Haas, Jr., the CEO of Levi Strauss. When we were on a fishing trip one day, he told me about how unhappy he was that they made the move. I had my eye on the property across the street now known as Levi's Plaza, so I said, "Wally, why don't we do something?" That conversation launched an entire odyssey. At the end of that journey, Levi Strauss moved out here and the project that Gyo designed for us became known as Levi's Plaza. It is now the corporate headquarters of Levi Strauss.

I cannot remember the intimate details about choosing the architect, but I do know that Gyo was the architect of choice. Mr. Haas, Jr., was on the Board of Directors of the Ford Foundation. The Foundation had an atrium building on the East Side of New York. Mr. Haas felt that design would bring back "the family feeling." I do not remember exactly how I met Gyo, but I got to know him and I think that our personalities clicked. He had the design of the National Air and Space Museum to his credit, which was impressive; but other than that, I was not acquainted with Gyo's work.

The most exciting part of the project for me was its totality. We had our eye on the land. There had been an historical assemblage of the land made up of a lot of different owners. Someone had the idea for a massive furniture mart and used the Travelers Insurance Company

ABOVE The brick face and scale complement existing structures
RIGHT The plaza faces the bay and is open and inviting

to help them assemble it. It became Travelers' own Vietnam. Travelers had invested in it, got in, and could not get out. I knew of the need for Travelers to sell it and the need of Levi Strauss to find a site and construct a building. Everything came together. I was able to buy the land from Travelers and we had enough land to create a plaza with the open space in the park.

The difficult part was when it came time to negotiate the deal. Levi Strauss was a public company. Mr. Haas made it abundantly clear that he had to represent the shareholders and it could not be a personal or emotional decision. I do remember how we had to make the case that from an economic standpoint, relocating to a new site would not cost them any more than staying in their building. We were able to accomplish that.

Embarcadero Center was very inefficient. There was a tremendous load factor because of the relatively small floor plates. We had a much more efficient load factor and were able to equate the rent per usable foot—equal to or better than Embarcadero Center. It became a natural. It worked out economically for Levi; it worked for us. We brought in a partner, the Equitable Life Insurance Company. It was a win-win for all parties.

We wanted to create a place with a meaningful identity because of the historical nature of the neighborhood and we wanted the buildings to try to reflect the character

of the neighborhood. As a result of that, we went with the brick exterior walls. The idea for the park evolved out of the design process. When we saw the first design, we liked it right away.

I remember looking at the steel work in the atrium and reflecting on the original call of an architect to paint the steel white. That just seemed wrong. Levi had an architect that represented them—Howard Friedman. He said, "Why don't we paint the steelwork in the ceiling blue, the Levi denim blue?" We took Howard's advice.

Sometimes there are confrontations between the developer and architect on a project. When an architect digs in his heels on an issue and the developer does the same, getting a resolution can be a challenge. I don't remember those kinds of disagreements while working on Levi's Plaza. The project went quite smoothly.

This building and Levi's Plaza are next to a neighborhood association called Telegraph Hill Dwellers Association. I defy anybody in America to find people more concerned and more able to fight battles at City Hall. I defy anyone to find another neighborhood group more interested in limiting their environment, protecting traffic flow and all the issues neighborhoods have. Gyo's office, with Bill Valentine, was able to navigate the guarded waters of this vigilant group in a very fine fashion.

Gyo is a total gentleman, first rate and clearly a good designer and a good architect. Working with Bill Valentine and Mark Otsea, who was under Bill, was a first-rate experience. We brought in Arthur Gensler & Associates to do the interiors and the two firms worked very well together.

Gyo and HOK also worked with landscape architect Lawrence Halprin. We had the usual constraints of city zoning, but by finding a way for the city, Gyo, and Larry Halprin to work together, we were able to create a wonderful new park. We had to get a variance from the city, and we got the variance for the buildings largely because of the park.

Allan Temko, a Pulitzer Prize winning architecture critic, called Levi's Plaza a "gift to the city." We are pleased that Allan's evaluation held up. Clearly part of the success of the Plaza is due to the seamless way it ties to the neighborhood. Levi's Plaza is considered to be one of the finest, if not the finest, office parks in the city. It is especially gratifying to see people use the park at lunch and to see tourists going by with guidebooks in hand.

Gerson Bakar is a developer in San Francisco.

DALLAS GALLERIA

DALLAS, TEXAS

I liked creating a center that is very dense so that people can easily move around and

enjoy it. In a way, it is much like a community center.

I worked with Gerald Hines, one of the most sophisticated developers who, early in his career, learned to hire good architects to design his projects. He is a quiet, unassuming person, trained as an engineer, who likes to be involved during the entire project. He is smart about his work and always builds upscale projects. Gerry is also very thoughtful, and never raises his voice.

Gerry called us for the Dallas Galleria project because we had done the Houston Galleria. We came up with a design approach and he accepted the idea. There was a lot of traffic, a major road on one side and a compact site—more so than the site of the Houston Galleria. We had to figure out how to provide for all the parking and the traffic movement. Because it was so dense, we had to study how to get the traffic in because a shopping center is all about movement of cars, parking, and people entering and getting around easily and efficiently.

The Dallas Galleria has four levels with a big ice rink in the middle, and is occupied by retail and high-fashion stores. Many office buildings and a major hotel are attached. In Dallas, we had a lot more control over the architecture,

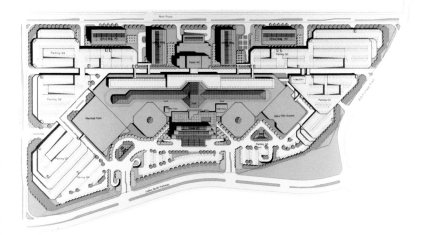

the garages, and so forth. In Houston, parts were added and some of that we could not control. So architecturally, I think Dallas is more interesting. Also, after doing one Galleria, we tried to refine the second one.

We really wanted to help Gerry create an important center in North Dallas that would draw people. There was a lot of potential and it turned into a success for that area. This particular community of buildings is more interesting than a typical mall. With its shopping, offices, and hotels, it is a city in itself.

GERALD D. HINES: COLLABORATION AND COMMUNICATION

I think part of the responsibility of an architect, even though he is not a programmer, is to suggest ways to mitigate some of the risks faced by the owner or developer.

I found the Dallas project to be very interesting. We had, of course, a proven record in Houston, and so we could improve on the details of this development, which we did, because of our financial backing. We introduced and integrated the office buildings and the hotel, allowing each of those entities its own individual image. We also refined the drop-off and circulation, improving accessibility.

We worked in sessions, usually every month, in order to bring the project together. Then it was put into detailed drawings and working drawings. We were on a very fast-track system. We used precast beams to build the structures.

Gyo is very soft spoken, thoughtful, and imaginative. He is willing to address all the challenges of any project, the aesthetics as well as the cost of the construction materials, in order to achieve the desired design. He is a wonderful person with whom to work.

It's the character and the imagination of each individual architect that will either strike a chord with the developer or not. I think Gyo is an outstanding, world-class architect who ranks with the very best, in addition to being a person of great integrity and very pleasant.

Gerald D. Hines is the founder and Chairman of Hines Interests, a real estate development firm.

LEFT A disinctive skyline with defined, separate entrances
RIGHT The glass skylight and ice rink run along the central spine

GYO OBATA: ON A MONUMENTAL GATEWAY

We wanted the airport to be a gateway to this country and its capital city.

The King and the royal family of Saudi Arabia hired Bechtel Corporation to oversee the building of a new airport, later named the King Khaled International Airport. After they interviewed several firms, they selected HOK, which had experience in airport design, to work with Bechtel. In a sense, Bechtel was our client, but we presented to King Fahd bin Abdul Aziz.

The Saudis designated 70,000 acres in Riyadh for airport development. The master plan included four terminals: two domestic and two international. A Royal Terminal would serve the King, his royal family and special visitors. In addition, we also designed a huge, hexagonal mosque for up to 5,000 worshippers.

In order to build this airport, we researched the history of Islamic architecture and called in a knowledgeable consultant. The mosque and terminal designs emerged from that research. While the building is contemporary, there are references to Islamic architecture. We also researched appropriate graphics to use in the mosque. In creating this gateway to the capital and the Kingdom, we imbued the buildings with monumentality. When people go through them, they feel the importance of entering the country.

At most airports, once people land they go through customs and then walk through endless corridors to claim their luggage. We wanted to make the entry point to Saudi Arabia welcoming. We created a garden oasis in the center of the terminal building. Arriving travelers stroll past plants and flowers, proceed through customs, and enter the country. A series of clerestory windows in geometric forms offers controlled, natural light.

After working on this large project, I realized that my Cranbrook education under Eliel Saarinen was very helpful. Saarinen always talked about the bigger picture. He had each of his graduate students work on city planning. That experience gave me the confidence to take on a large project such as this.

MILDRED F. SCHMERTZ: AN IMMENSE, LUXURIOUS COMPLEX

I thought "surprise, surprise" that anything so immense could have been

so well put together.

I wrote a feature about this airport for the March, 1984 issue of *Architectural Record,* after going to Riyadh for the opening ceremonies. I had the good fortune of being in the company of Gyo and the late Bill Remington, who at the time headed the public relations activities of HOK. In all my years at the magazine, he was the most persevering and effective liaison between the firm he represented and those of us he hoped would produce a favorable story. He visited our office more regularly than anyone else I can remember, and I believed that getting HOK published in *Record* was all he cared about. I was wrong. One day he

invited me to his New York City office and there on his wall were dozens of framed covers from magazines of every sort—engineering, construction, petroleum, schools, medical facilities, industrial plants—and the subject of each cover was an HOK building. For Bill, our magazine had never been the only game in town.

Nevertheless, he had decided that this airport belonged in *Record* and he offered it exclusively to us. I think I was the only member of the staff who actually wanted to go to Saudi Arabia, even though, like everyone else, I knew that women were not allowed to travel alone there, and were discriminated against in many ways. Bill got me a hard won visa and promised that he and HOK would take good care of me. "Everything is going to be okay," he said, so I went.

Gyo and Bill were on the plane in first class, I was in tourist. Bill came to the back of the plane from time to time to bring me first-class treats. We arrived in Riyadh at night and began to go through customs and be checked by the authorities. I was suddenly stopped and put in a waiting pen with other women who were not supposed to be admitted because they were not wives. According to Saudi custom, a man could bring in his wife because she was his property, but couldn't just bring a woman. Gyo and Bill had to explain to a Saudi airport official that I was essential to their work, and after about an hour of pleading, they got me through.

We showed up at the hotel where I had a reservation, but the desk clerk would not admit me as a woman by myself. Bill said to Gyo, "Okay, so what do we do with Mildred?" HOK had a housing compound in Riyadh so they

LEFT Arriving passengers have a clear view of the airport's scale
RIGHT Wide plazas and water features create a grand entrance

went to the phone to find me a place there. While they were gone, I got good news from the desk clerk. The hotel, fortunately, was part of an Indian-owned international chain, the guests came from all over the world, and the management was not strictly bound by Saudi custom. The clerk, an Indian, told me I could have my room that night if HOK would produce the necessary authorization the next day. Bill was able to do this and the room was secure for my entire stay.

I was not allowed to attend the opening ceremonies at the airport, but Bill and Gyo took me anyway. I had tried to get an invitation well in advance, but never received a response. When we arrived, the men were allowed to go into the grand hall for the ceremonies followed by a splendid lunch, but I had to stay, unfed, in a smaller adjoining space with the women and children. We watched the event on television. The next day, HOK made amends by giving me a complete tour of the airport complex. We went by car from place to place, and these were long rides. I was shown everything: the two international terminals, the pair of domestic terminals, the mosque at the core of the master plan, and the royal terminal off by itself. We visited the King's private quarters in this terminal, and saw his immense royal bathtub.

A project this immense and extensive, designed within a unified structural, geometric, and modular system, is a phenomenon in the world of architecture. One might think that this consistency might be monotonous and boring, but HOK developed many variants of the basic systems to create an imposing and exciting variety of forms throughout. This project was far more elaborate and extensive than any of HOK's previous work had been. An architectural firm almost never gets a commission from a client with such massive financial resources, nor does it ever have complete design control. HOK was given carte blanche to design the grandest airport on the planet to bring wonder and excitement for all who come and go—perhaps eventually for even the women. I am glad I went to see it, and will never forget the trip, or Bill Remington. He kept his promise that everything would be okay for me and I had a fine time. Now that more than 25 years have passed since that adventure, I realize that looking after me in a place like Saudi Arabia could not have been easy for him. Thanks for the memory, Bill.

Mildred F. Schmertz was an editor and writer at *Architectural Record* for 33 years. From 1985 to her retirement in 1990 she was editor-in-chief. She is currently a contributing writer for *Architectural Digest*.

KING SAUD UNIVERSITY

RIYADH, SAUDI ARABIA

GYO OBATA: A NEW COMMUNITY IN A DESERT

Seeing the whole new community come from nothing, the influence of the regional architecture, the materials, the movement, the use of controlled daylight—that was exciting.

During a recession in the 1970s, George Hellmuth heard that the Saudis were about to build a university in Riyadh. He and I traveled to Saudi Arabia and presented to the president of the university and his right-hand person, a Pakistani engineer. After the interview, we were awarded the job, our first overseas venture.

The project site was outside of Riyadh, in total desert. The Saudis wanted us to envision what the university should be. We contacted an educational consultant to devise a whole program, including the classes to be taught. I brought in Harvard scholar Oleg Grabar, a leading authority on Islamic architecture, to guide us. Symbolism is important in Islamic architecture. We researched the programs for the large university, without much input from the client, who told us that we were the experts. Our educational consultant from Caudill Rowlett Scott (CRS) helped establish the academic direction.

Climate was a significant factor in the design. Because of the hot sun, we enclosed everything except for the main corridor. In the central area, I placed the library, the main theatre, the student center, and the administrative offices. From there, I had spines that went to the liberal arts area and the science area. Because this was a desert and we could not tunnel into the ground, I put all the utilities on the ground level spine and a major walkway on the next level, so that people could walk up or down in a three-story building. The buildings are close together for shading purposes. The major circulation is in the spine that leads to a secondary spine into each college.

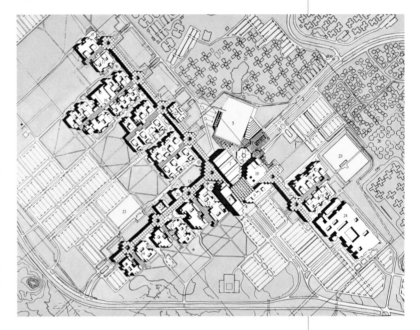

We knew steel would be hard to get, so we went with precast concrete and made it on site. We designed all precast walkways. The concrete is a beautiful beige-colored precast, recalling the old structures that existed in Riyadh.

This was one of HOK's biggest projects, built by a combination of an American contractor and a French contractor, and with South Korean labor. Within a year, we designed and did the working drawings, but it took much longer to build. The whole idea of ease of movement, separation of disciplines, the effects of climate, and creation of diffused lighting inspired the design.

MILDRED SCHMERTZ: OBSERVING CULTURE, SCALE, AND ORDER

HOK is too good to have a signature touch.

My second trip to Saudi Arabia under the sponsorship of HOK was to visit this desert campus, a few miles from the outskirts of Riyadh. The feature I wrote after the visit appeared in the April 1986 issue of *Architectural Record.* Once again I flew in with Gyo and others of his team, including, of course, Bill Remington. On this trip, HOK was supposed to present to the airport authorities a letter on my behalf from the president of the university. Whoever was to take care of this detail didn't, so I was stopped as before, but not again ordered to wait in the unwanted women's pen. I considered this progress. HOK made a call to the university, the authorization was soon given, I was allowed into the country, and there was no trouble at the hotel this time.

The university has much in common with the airport. There is a geometric order, a structural order, a landscape order and an order of scale. Like the airport, the university is immense, but its basic elements are compactly arranged to reduce walking distances; in contrast, the airport terminals are spaced miles apart. The university was designed for 15,000 to 20,000 male students. Today's student body is much larger and female students can be found in the School of Nursing and other related medical and health-care disciplines. The campus comprises 6.5 million square feet of building area, covers 3.5 square miles, and uses 85,000 individual architectural and structural precast-concrete elements manufactured on the site. Construction took almost four years.

I interviewed the president of the university and various faculty members, all of whom were men educated in Europe or America. None wanted to talk about the architecture specifically, nor were they much interested in the fabrication of the precast concrete structure. What excited them was the fact that the university had actually happened, that the many different schools, different subjects, and new faculties were there. I think they were amazed and surprised that an entire university could be planned, constructed, and begin to function in such a short period of time. So, of course, was I. Unfortunately, when I made this visit 24 years ago, women were invisible. In the interior of one of the buildings, I saw a walled-off section with a narrow horizontal slot of a window. Out of sight behind it were female clerical workers, none of whom were

LEFT, RIGHT Covered, pedestrian walkways protect users from the hot sun

allowed to encounter the university males. Their clerical work was passed to them through the window by a male clerk, and collected there when completed.

Paris-based weaver Sheila Hicks and sculptor Daniel Graffin designed and installed the major artwork in principal locations throughout the campus. At the time of the King Khaled International Airport dedication, my HOK friends had a celebrity they wanted me to meet, but they would not say who. They took me to the compound in the desert where those who worked at the construction site of the university lived. Hicks and Graffin each had a studio there. Sheila, who had become an internationally recognized artist, knew me as a fellow student at the Yale art school, but we had not been in touch for many years.

Bill Remington and HOK architect Bill Valentine told her that they were bringing me to the compound to see the designs she was making for the tapestries that would decorate the university. The three decided that seeing her would be a happy surprise for me, and indeed it was.

We both found it amazing to meet again in the desert of Saudi Arabia, but arranging the event was typical of the thoroughness of HOK's effort to help me understand the scope and depth of their architecture. I continue to be filled with wonder that any architectural firm could simultaneously master plan, design, engineer, and build so well two such vast developments in a desert.

KELLOGG COMPANY HEADQUARTERS

BATTLE CREEK, MICHIGAN

GYO OBATA: BRINGING COMMUNITIES TOGETHER

Total design responsibility—from the site to the building to the art and interiors!

That is very unusual.

Kellogg was a challenging project because of the division between Battle Creek's city and suburb. Bill LaMothe, the President, said he would build a new headquarters downtown if the suburb and the city would unify as one—Kellogg was the town's biggest employer. There was a vote and the idea was accepted.

Bill and his people selected a site near the Battle Creek River. They wanted a new environment for Kellogg that would attract young management people to the area. Many retail stores had gone to the suburbs and they hoped the new headquarters would help revive the city.

HOK interviewed for and was awarded the project. Bill LaMothe had some fascinating ideas. He wanted a multi-level structure with escalators on which people could interact freely as they moved through the building. In keeping with his vision, we placed an atrium in the middle, with two wings, escalators, and a big skylight. It was a space with greenery where people could move around. On the ground level, we designed an attractive dining facility for people to enjoy. The design also included a beautiful garden looking out on the river and a jogging track. I asked Italian sculptor Constantino Nivola to do an abstract piece about a family. I also requested that my wife, Courtney Bean Obata, create a series of terra-cotta tile murals depicting the nature of food. After all, Kellogg is in the food product business.

Our comprehensive project responsibilities included designing the building and landscaping, and selecting the

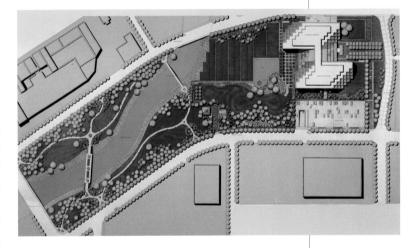

artwork, furniture, colors and fabrics, exhibits, and even the silverware. Chip Reay, a graphic designer with HOK, did a timeline study of Kellogg. We traveled to Battle Creek often for incredible discussion sessions. Architecture is a process of change, and we worked together to find the right solutions. I thoroughly enjoyed working with Bill and appreciated his keen interest in the project and attentiveness to each detail.

The Kellogg project gave Battle Creek a sense of place. The local people appreciated the new headquarters' park-like atmosphere. The project unified two communities and created a live-work-play environment that attracted professionals.

BILL LAMOTHE: BUILDING A COMMITMENT TO THE FUTURE

We met throughout the whole process. We had a committee on which I participated. I wanted it to be right. We traveled to St. Louis and the HOK folks came often to see us. It wasn't difficult because we were excited about what was happening. It all came together and we were pleased with the result. It was like hitting a home run!

For about 12 years, I was the Chief Executive Officer, President, and Chairman of the Kellogg Company. I became the CEO and Chairman in 1979. In the late '70s, we were doing business with about 130 countries and wanting to expand, but had difficulty attracting professional people to our small community.

Battle Creek is a company town and we were the biggest employer. Professional people do not like that kind of atmosphere. They want to be in a community with good schools and a sizeable university. So we made a decision, with the Board's approval, that we would move our headquarters to Chicago or Atlanta. We argued that we could travel to work more quickly out of those areas than we could in Battle Creek.

Some of the founding fathers of the community thought our moving would be a terrible blow. They said, "Mr. Kellogg started the company here. His brother built the sanitarium. They were well known." We said, "Here is our problem. You folks have tried repeatedly to bring in some of the townships, but they never vote to come into the city because they know their taxes will rise." At that time, we were a city of 35,000 and the largest neighboring township had about 25,000 people.

After a lot of debate, we decided that if we could get the township and city to merge, we would have at least a working population on which to build. We were written up in *Fortune* as the company that held the gun to their community because we were resolved to move our headquarters if the city and township would not merge.

There were six months of very difficult times. People in the township were angry. We knew the city people would vote to merge because their taxes would go down while

RIGHT An entrance atrium placed between two office wings

the township people's taxes would go up. People called me at home and threatened my family because they felt the company was forcing the community to vote for something that would increase thousands of people's taxes. They were emotional. I installed more security at home to protect my wife and six children. It was a worrisome time, but the measure passed.

Then we faced the dilemma of what to do about our company headquarters. We pondered whether to move out on the highway running between Detroit and Chicago. The Board suggested we "bite the bullet" and put the headquarters right in the middle of the city, so the people would see our commitment to the community. We then began interviewing architects who would pick up the spirit of what we were doing.

When Gyo and HOK came in, they understood what we were trying to do. We wanted a headquarters that was more than a palace. We wanted something practical that would fit the size of the community and be well done. Gyo persuaded us to look at HOK's project for Levi Strauss in San Francisco. That caught our attention. It was not grandiose, and it was very well done. He also took us to Detroit, where he had done some work, and to Cranbrook, where he had gone to school. The facilities there resembled Frank Lloyd Wright's work. We liked that. After much debate, we said, "Let's go with HOK's thinking on the design," and we worked with them for a number of months.

Gyo captured what we were trying to do. We were basically a food company, and we wanted to have the architecture and the treatment inside focus on what we were all about. Gyo and his people met with us often. I

spent a lot of time on the project because we planned to be there for at least the next 50 years and we wanted it to be right. Gyo understood that, and we appreciated his ideas about what the building's interior and exterior should look like.

In a four-story, spread-out building, we did not like the idea of elevators that would whisk people off to their floors and to their offices. We wanted our people to be able to see each other. So we decided that in the center core, we would have escalators to move people up and down on every floor and serve as the hub. We did have elevators as well, so if people needed a lift, they could take one up. The escalators became the central focal point with other things built around them, such as the glass treatments and replications of wheat and the various grains with which we worked. I was very much involved in this.

In 1986, we moved in. For a few days, we opened the building to the entire community so that people could walk through and see it. Today, the building still looks like it opened just a couple of years ago. It has been a wonderful headquarters for the company and it has complemented the city. We have not turned the city of Battle Creek around entirely, but it is a much stronger community. The schools are better and the business community is healthier. A lot of things came out of this whole approach that Gyo had much to do with.

Gyo is a thoughtful person who showed great sensitivity toward what we were trying to accomplish. He grabbed onto the project, introduced ideas that helped shape our "dream," and had the chemistry to work well with us. I read the history of Frank Lloyd Wright and about some of the problems that people had dealing with him. He was such a strong-willed character. People who were paying to have a Frank Lloyd Wright building or house designed and built were to appreciate whatever he created for them. Gyo was much more focused on, "What does this client really want to have happen here?" He is a quiet, gentle soul who is awfully good at what he does. Working with Gyo and HOK was a terrific experience.

I think Gyo would walk away from a situation if he was uncomfortable with what a client wanted, or did not feel it was right for HOK. He has the courage to say, "I think another architect would better serve your needs." He is unique in my judgment.

The most exciting part of the project happened toward the end when I saw the various pieces fit together. It was not just the construction and the thoughtfulness that went into it, but also the focus on the artwork, furniture, and fixtures that were included. It was all a part of the whole program and, as it fell in place and came together, we said, "This is it. You've got it. You're right on the mark." We were very excited about how it turned out.

The building helped us to communicate better than we had in the past and to keep people apprised of where we were headed. As a company, we became much closer to our employees. If we went for a coffee break or lunch, we took the escalator down and interacted with all kinds of people. We also improved our focus on fitness and health, which our company has historically emphasized with great grains, good foods, and a solid breakfast.

Over the years, the first floor of our new headquarters has served as a place for special community programs and projects. The building has fulfilled our hope that the community would actively use it. So it turned out to be what we hoped it to be—something the community would be proud of and in which they could play a part. The headquarters is not an Empire State Building. It is only four stories tall in a community with few high-rise buildings. It fits in quietly, and yet, its landscaping and property all blend in very well with downtown Battle Creek.

After the building went up, the most vocal person in the township against it suddenly called and wanted to see me. My secretary met him at the front door and brought him up the escalator, pointing out different things. He gave me a package that contained an aerial photo of the building and the downtown area. It was quite attractive. He apologized for being so obstinate about our project. When he saw it completed, he realized that the community had indeed come together. He was glad that we persevered. That took courage and character. From then on, we became at least passing friends.

Our employees were proud of our accomplishment in bringing the community together. We were committed to the future and to making Battle Creek one of the best small Midwestern cities in the country. That was evident in our commitment to things like the United Way and in our employees' contributions to and participation in other community activities like the 5K runs for a cancer cure.

I am proud of my long career at Kellogg, and to have had the opportunity to help bring that community together for the future. I am grateful to have worked closely with Gyo to deliver a building that is a community focal point. All of that gives me a profound sense of accomplishment.

William E. LaMothe is the retired Chief Executive Officer, President, and Chairman of the Kellogg Company.

GYO OBATA: TRADITIONS THAT INFORM DESIGN

For architects, a place of worship presents an intriguing challenge. Our goal is to create an environment in which spatial qualities and light levels connect the etheric and earthly realms, inspire people in their sacred practice, and move them to return, again and again.

Someone in our office may have been a member of B'nai Amoona and told us that the congregation was moving from University City westward into St. Louis County. They were leaving a synagogue designed by Erich Mendelsohn, a very famous Jewish architect. Rabbi Bernard Lipnick thought that someone Jewish with an understanding of the faith ought to design the new building. Before he would choose an architect, he asked to talk to me.

I held long conversations with the Rabbi. I told him that while I did not belong to the Jewish faith, I would try to understand his vision and requirements for the building and would work closely with him. He gave me books to read regarding the history, practices, traditions, and nuances of the Jewish faith. He invited me to a seder, where I spent an evening with his family and friends. Rabbi Lipnick thought that was a good introduction to Judaism.

After he spoke with me at length, the Rabbi felt comfortable with me. One interesting thing I learned is that the Jewish religion focuses on life on Earth. Rabbi Lipnick did not want the synagogue to be a soaring building that embraced the heavens, like many of the Christian churches. But the idea of light was important, so we have clerestory lighting.

In the geometry of the building, we had to create an intimate main sanctuary that could be expanded. The synagogue design needed to accommodate both regular services, and High Holiday services, so we incorporated movable walls that could essentially double the space for attending members. HOK Project Manager Bob Schwartz facilitated our understanding of the design ramifications.

This project posed quite a challenge for me because an architecturally significant Mendelsohn building had been B'nai Amoona's previous home. In designing this building, I wanted to fully understand and be sensitive to the requirements of the Jewish faith. My conversations with Rabbi Lipnick became a highlight of the project, and led to the design.

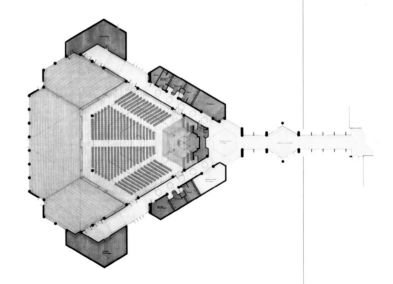

RABBI BERNARD LIPNICK, Ph.D.: TRADITIONS AND TRANSITIONS

Wow! There are not many church structures in the world as beautiful as this, on as striking a setting as the piece of land on which it sits. I think it is stunning.

The congregation of B'nai Amoona is 128 years old. It is a long-standing institution in this community and has called several different buildings home over the years. The most recent was a special building designed by German Jewish architect Erich Mendelsohn, who escaped Europe before World War II. Completed in 1950, the building has been on the itineraries of architecture schools around the country.

The building design incorporates a number of unique concepts including an expandable sanctuary, which became commonplace in churches and synagogues across the country. Mendelsohn achieved architectural fame with great buildings in this country and in Israel, where he designed the Hadassah Hospital, the Weizmann Institute, and others. When we occupied the building in University City, Missouri, we knew we were sitting on an architectural gem.

My calling in the rabbinate is education. I came to the congregation as the educational director, rather than as the Rabbi. In the 1960s and 1970s, the Jewish community was moving out of University City and farther west into Creve Coeur and St. Louis County. We were rapidly losing our kids and I had no intention of remaining in a congregation without children.

Deciding to move was a difficult decision. A lot of money was involved. We also had a sense of history and valued the University City building as an architectural gem. The main consideration was that the kids could not reach us. We did not have a Jewish day school that was acceptable to us. We were totally dependent upon afternoon, supplementary Jewish education, which we called "Hebrew School."

I also wanted to acquire a weekend retreat site and build an educational facility on the land. We purchased 33 acres on which to create a retreat center complete with playing fields for kids to spend weekends and summers, and a synagogue. It became clear that we would have to have everything together on the same site, including a sanctuary. I was assured that if we built the educational facility as cheaply as possible, the sanctuary would be "a jewel."

A committee composed of good, high-powered people who knew a lot about building and who cared about the congregation's future ran a design competition and asked

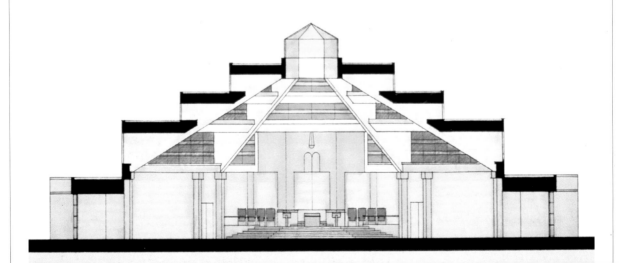

people to submit plans. There were some very famous names in the running—people who became known internationally.

In traditionally oriented congregations, people walk to services on the Sabbath. When Mendelsohn designed his building on Washington and Trinity, there was not a single parking space. On the street, there was parking for about 10 cars for a sanctuary that could hold 2,000 people. Our winning argument for this building was that there would be plenty of parking. We gave up the idea that people had to walk to services on the Sabbath. People could drive from anywhere, if there was parking. Consequently, this would be the last building that we would have to build.

I went to Israel, visited interesting buildings, and found an architect I liked—Zalman Enav. When it came down to decision-making time, I was told that my desire to bring an Israeli architect into the picture was a disaster waiting to happen. It didn't make sense to engage someone 6,000 miles away who was not familiar with building materials we use here. The committee preferred the proposal submitted by Gyo Obata.

I said, "No. To go from the Mendelsohn building, built by a survivor of the Holocaust, to a building built by a Japanese architect who is not even Jewish is unacceptable. We cannot have Obata design our building."

The committee acknowledged that as the Rabbi, I held the power of veto. They would not engage any architect I deemed unsuitable. But they asked me to at least meet with Gyo Obata and talk with him about it. I agreed.

Gyo came to see me and we had a conversation. I found out that he was a Nisei, a first generation Japanese American, that his parents had been incarcerated during the war, and that he, himself, later served in the United

States Army. We discussed my vision for the synagogue and the kind of Jewish culture that I wanted it to represent. I discovered that this man, with his Japanese background, was in step with my hopes and goals for this new building. We talked about the importance of symbols and symbolic action, and about the place of family in both the Japanese and Jewish cultures. I was struck by the similarities and felt I was talking with a kindred soul.

Gyo was uniquely suited to understand the position of the Jew, the purpose of the synagogue, the effects of persecution, and how those principles would translate into some kind of an architectural entity. Gyo said, "Let me

study Judaism." I gave him a pile of books and he left to go study. After several subsequent discussions, Gyo came up with this architectural motif.

There is a stained glass window visible from the building's back side. A building on Academy and Vernon in St. Louis, built in 1918, served our congregation prior to the Washington and Trinity building. I had never been in it, but my interest in architecture and our pending design prompted me to visit. The building was not in good shape and had been acquired by an African-American church. Reverend O'Hara gave me a tour of the building.

Two things impressed me: the upper halves of three stained glass windows (the lower halves had been stolen), and the building's cornerstone. It was a brick building with a white cornerstone that had been cemented over, possibly to conceal the Jewish Star and Hebrew writing inscribed there. I proposed to Reverend O'Hara my desire to buy the cornerstone. I offered to replace it with any cornerstone he liked. And I sought to procure the remaining stained glass windows, offering to replace them with stained glass windows of his choice. He agreed.

The day they removed the cornerstone, I was there. I knew there was an ancient custom when they laid a cornerstone. People would throw coins behind the cornerstone before they cemented the stone in place. I got those coins. We cleaned the cornerstone and it revealed the Star. The writing on the side said, "Congregation B'nai Amoona, June 18, 1918, organized in 1886." It is not perfect, but it became a centerpiece. I had these stained glass windows and the cornerstone in my possession during my interactions with the committee.

Gyo and I looked at the three beautiful stained glass windows of the three main figures. I don't know if that was what inspired him to think in terms of a hexagon, but he came up with a brilliant plan to make them the building's centerpiece. The hexagon, which is the Jewish Star, predominates. We approved the plan and began the building process.

I was always amazed at HOK's responsiveness. I have never worked with a more cooperative and helpful firm. I would make a telephone call to express a concern, a complaint or an observation, and in half an hour, a van with six people would show up to rectify the situation. Why would Mr. Obata have been so attentive? I was told Gyo wanted to create a signature Obata experience in St. Louis, and this was to be it.

The blessing of this building was not without loss. There is a special atmosphere when people walk, rather than drive, to their synagogue. We lost that, and we lost some people who decided to remain in University City to protect the integrity of that community. It was a difficult transition. B'nai Amoona was a serious participant in the culture of University City. Leaving that community was difficult.

When we moved from the Washington and Trinity building, it marked a halcyon era in our history. We had a long motorcade that carried The Scrolls of the Law on a big, 18-wheeler, flat-bed truck. Winston Churchill said, "We shape our dwellings; thereafter they shape us." Indeed, the building turned out to be a jewel, a precious stone in the shape of the Star of David. It is a very beautiful, inspiring, and spiritual place.

While no one has ever designed a perfect building, Mr. Obata came pretty close with B'nai Amoona. He designed a more Jewish building than most Jewish architects could design. It is a spiritual gem, a work of genius, and a worthy successor to Mendelsohn's building, which was my original purpose and hope.

Rabbi Bernard Lipnick, Ph.D., was Senior Rabbi of Congregation B'nai Amoona at the time of the project. He is now Rabbi Emeritus.

GYO OBATA: SPIRALING INTO INFINITY

The Temple in Independence is rather mystical. It went soaring up, going on to heaven. The head of the church at that time, Wallace B. Smith, was a direct descendant of Joseph Smith, Jr., the original founder. Joseph Smith had designated this specific site in Independence, Missouri, for the Temple.

We sent the Temple Architectural Committee photographs of churches that I had done. They selected three firms. I interviewed with church President Wallace B. Smith, and we got the job.

One of the church elders was a religious buildings scholar. He wrote an elaborate program. People entered the church through a long, dimly lit corridor, sparsely decorated with religious symbols. The effect of moving through this rising passageway was to clear their minds. Suddenly, the entire sanctuary would open up before them.

The church members call themselves a "Community of Christ" and project a worldwide mission for the church. They were a young church and wanted an identity free of other influences such as Gothic or Georgian. I had the opportunity to create something entirely new for them. As I thought about their worldwide ministry, the idea of a conical shell form came to me.

I showed two designs, and they chose the spiral form. Building it required a mathematical formula for design. The proportion of the church from the exterior wall as it spiraled 300 feet required many computer drawings so the contractor could get the exact size. Bob Stockdale, my assistant on this project, was a computer wizard and he helped the contractor with our drawings.

Building the structure posed a challenge. Concrete was too difficult, so we made a stick building—steel, covered on the inside with plaster. On the outside, we used a metal roof and granite on the walls. It was a major architectural and engineering feat. For the roof, we worked with A. Zahner Company the sheet metal people who do many of Frank Gehry's metal skins. J.E. Dunn Construction Company of Kansas City also contributed greatly to this building's success.

The main seating in this house of worship is on the floor, with additional seating in the balcony. As people look up to the ceiling, it spirals into infinity. Because the shape was very difficult with the curving and reflectivity, we worked with acoustical engineers to ensure that the worshipper could hear the sermon and music.

Creating a Temple for this group was really challenging and rewarding. It is right in the heart of Independence, Missouri. Its soaring edifice is visible for miles around.

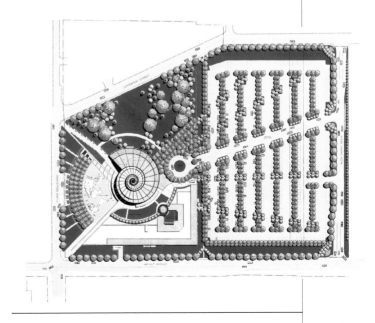

LEFT A spiral-shaped church draws worshippers inside to the soaring interior

ALAN D. TYREE: A SIMPLE, TRANQUIL, AND TIMELESS SANCTUARY

It was the first time in history they were able to design this—so many pieces of steel—the complexity of the spiral constantly changing.

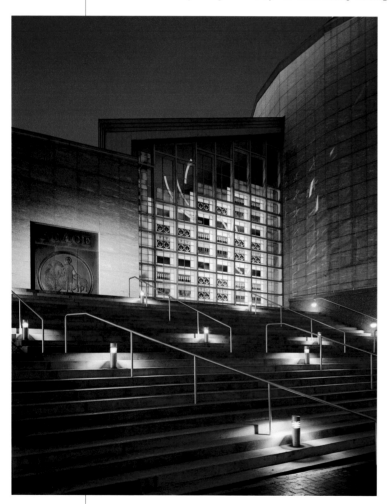

I chaired the Temple Architectural Committee, which later evolved into the Temple Art Committee. I had already become acquainted with Gyo and many other architects around the country. We focused on who was to be the design architect, not the firm alone. In fact we had an architect on our staff conduct a rigorous study, which outlined for us a rubric to determine who we could get. Maybe 50 or 60 firms contacted us to express interest, but half of them dropped out when they saw the forms we sent them, as they knew they would not qualify.

One of the questions we raised was, "What volume of business in terms of dollars has your firm done during the past 12 months?" We wanted to know what they were capable of doing. I went along with other committee members to see the work these architects had achieved. We traveled all around the country and to Scandinavia. Our committee narrowed the list to three.

We presented the three to a larger Temple Construction Committee, of which I was also a member, and asked them to help us. The finalists came back for a second presentation to our committee. They then returned for a third presentation before the larger committee. The larger committee said they did not feel we should make the decision and preferred that the church president, being the prophet of the church, the one with the spiritual insight for the Temple and its function, make the final decision.

Wallace P. Smith said to Howard S. Sheehey, Jr., and me, "I am not going to make this decision alone. You two are

LEFT Grand stairs lead to the doors of bronze and the church seal

going to have to help me." The three of us then visited the finalists in their offices. After our visits, we decided that Gyo was the unanimous choice. It seemed that we were in tune with him and he was the one who would best be able to do the work for us. Wherever we looked at his buildings, we saw a very good, imaginative spirit.

During a world conference that was an eight-day event, we had a service on a Tuesday night. There were people present who had dug down deeply into their pockets, along with their friends and relatives. Even poverty-stricken people from Haiti contributed. Prior to the service, we introduced Gyo to the fundraising people who headed up the drive in all areas of the church.

In the auditorium, there were about 100 seats reserved for us. By the time we finished our banquet and came over, those seats were gone. As luck would have it, my wife and I arrived at the same time that Gyo and his architectural team were coming through the doors. There were five in their party. One of them was Bob Stockdale, who did most of the drawings. Another was Rodney Leibold, the supervisor of construction. I looked up and saw the choir seats and said to Gyo and his group, "Just follow me." So there we sat and Gyo could look into the faces of all the people. It was a beautiful service, so intense with meaning, and everybody was so excited about the Temple.

Gyo was not introduced at that service, but was introduced at one of the conference business sessions and to the fundraisers. Nevertheless, he could look directly into the congregation. I noticed that Gyo's finger was kind of doing a spiral. As he was doing that, I did not think anything of it, but when I got home, I asked my wife Gladys, "Did you notice what Gyo was drawing?" She said, "Yes, he was doing whorls or circles on his program with his index finger." Later, when we were into the whole project,

I asked Gyo if he was aware of what he was doing with his finger on the program. He said that it was not a habit of his. Typically he sketched things.

We told Gyo our specifications. It was not an architectural program, but it was, nonetheless, a design program. We set certain things. Being an international body, we did not want the Temple to look like an American building. We wanted a building that would last for a century or two, or three, or four and not be locked in on the 20th century. Additionally, we did not want the building over-designed with opulence, so that people from the poorest or richest country in the world would feel comfortable and at home. We wanted a simple structure.

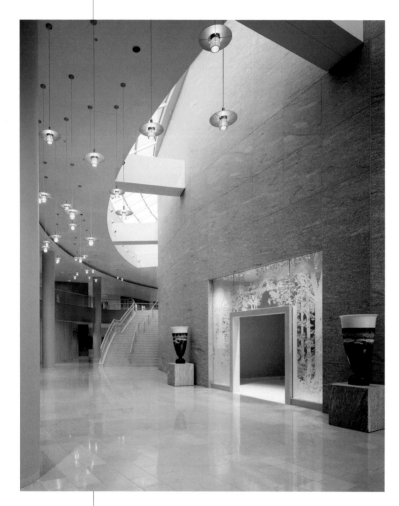

And we wanted something that people could identify with, something that reflected their homeland, some kind of universal symbol. We also told Gyo that the Temple would be dedicated to the pursuit of peace.

Gyo gave thought to that and came to us with three designs. The one he hoped that we would accept, he told us later, was the spiral, the reflection of the seashell. When people look down on it, it looks like a nautilus. When they look at it directly, it looks like a cone. It references other spirals: pine cones, nebulae, nature, the swirl of water. So, with the help of a computer, he discovered a universal symbol that was simple and feasible. I thought it had real possibility and so did the others. It did not take very long, after talking with Gyo, for us to decide. There was no criticism of the design among our leaders at all. The vast majority of our membership could identify with the concept and later we had the architectural drawings to share with everyone.

I guess the biggest surprise was how easily the project came together. On other building projects, we always had headaches and even some major problems with the architects or construction teams. This project had none of that. I have never worked with a more harmonious group of people. Of course, we encountered difficulties, but we worked them all out. None of them proved to be any kind of major hurdle or challenge. Starting with the design architect and his team, we had nothing but excellent relationships the whole time.

Gyo is such an unassuming man, which masks his true nature. He is ingenious. He is a quiet man who doesn't say much, but when he does speak, it's important. Those are

his areas of real eloquence, of course. People would not immediately recognize the genius, unless they were looking for it and until it expressed itself. Once it is apparent, then there is no mystery.

I lived with the excitement of the whole project from beginning to end. The first excitement was that we had raised the funds before the architect was hired. Within two years, we had the money. Two years later, we had the drawings under Gyo's capable leadership. And two years after that, we had the building thanks to the work of J.E. Dunn. They were tremendous to work with. And we had a program set up all the way through that was totally cost effective. We worked so closely with the architects and contractors that we knew what our costs were going to be. If we ran into anything we wanted to upgrade or downgrade, we could always work it out and stay within budget. We finished under budget. We had incentives for completion of the work, so we finished ahead of schedule.

What we anticipated has been fulfilled in many ways. For example, when people go into the space, they come up the worshippers' path. They are spiraling upward, climbing. As they ascend and it becomes bright with light, they have opportunities for worship because of the nature of the artwork that is there. They finally enter into the sanctuary, to the openness of that space, and then participate in the worship experience. The spiral itself symbolizes the spirit of God as it descends downward to meet the people in the sanctuary. In that environment, everything is conducive to the worship experience. I have been deeply moved there.

Almost everyone who comes to the Temple is somewhat awed by several elements: the tranquility, the peaceful atmosphere, and the beautiful simplicity. It is not the kind of beauty that astounds so much, but it is intrinsically

beautiful in its simplicity. It doesn't require ornamentation to be beautiful and it so well reflects elements of the natural world.

The Temple has not yet completely fulfilled the intention we have for it. We have to grow into it. Our church is just beginning to understand some of the real value of its message. Its importance is not local; its message is worldwide.

Alan D. Tyree was a member of the Temple Project Executive Committee and the Temple Project Committee. He chaired the Temple Architectural Committee that later evolved into the Temple Art Committee. The Temple is dedicated to peace.

Light and color are inseparable. For this project I felt inspired to introduce a spectrum of color because of the bright Florida sun. When the sun looks deeply into a color, it sees itself, and both radiate the bold delight of that discovery.

This was my first experience designing an aquarium. I drew some designs on a napkin which intrigued Jim Stuart, the client. He asked us to work with the firm Esherick Homsey Dodge and Davis from San Francisco. Jim valued their knowledge and experience building aquariums.

Every project has its own requirements and distinctive characteristics that inform the architecture. The aquarium design needed to incorporate complex technical specifications. The engineers who addressed these complex issues collaborated well with our team. The aquarium people shared their expertise about creating and maintaining an aquarium. Throughout the process, I learned a new technical language and new techniques.

Building an aquarium posed the interesting challenge of wrapping an environment around a living world of fish and plant material. We wanted people to experience the natural world's many habitats as they moved progressively through the building. The story begins in a cave area, winds its way past the aquifers and up through the building, enters a beach area, and then concludes in swamp land.

I liked thinking about the aquarium's relationship to Florida's natural world—the water, the wetlands, and the tropical regions. The idea of creating the greenhouse, wetland, and tropical settings on top of the building inspired the rooftop shell design. From there, visitors descend as though they are flowing with the water itself. In this building, the storyline of the exhibits and the circulation are inextricably linked.

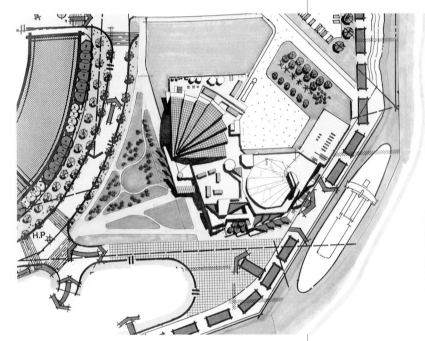

The building's exterior radiates vivid reds, blues, and yellows. Given the sun's intensity, we were able to use bright colors selected by me and my wife, Courtney. The interior of the three-story glass structure is dark and cannot have much daylight as people walking through prefer the darkness for viewing the exhibits. This provides a challenge to architectural expression.

I enjoyed working on The Florida Aquarium with a conscientious team committed to doing a great job. Together, we created an urban asset for the Tampa region and an inviting destination for tourists.

LEFT The shell-shaped aquarium forms a glass atrium and greenhouse

JIM STUART: NATURE'S CHURCH

The Florida Aquarium creates visual interest with its signature curly, twisty shape designed to fit around something organic and growing. Capped with a shell form that opens to the light, it offers an architectural expression of Florida and the natural world.

After Princeton, the U.S. Navy, and Harvard, I spent 18 years in a variety of business assignments. I came to Tampa, Florida, from Chicago, to run a business I had acquired. I ran into a buzzsaw with the former owner, ended up leaving the company, and spent a year looking for a new business to acquire.

One morning, a new friend, Bill Crown, Chairman of the Clearwater Aquarium, took me fishing. He said, "Jim, you do not want to do another business; you want to do an aquarium." He had developed some very preliminary plans

for an aquarium across the bay in Tampa. They had no idea how to fund it or how much it would actually cost, and they needed an executive director. This was a dream Bill had and it was not hard for me to catch the excitement.

At the time, Boston had one of the first great urban aquariums. Baltimore's came about 10 years later. The newest, most exciting one opened in Monterey, California, during the mid-'80s. Pardon the pun, but it was the "age of aquariums." The aquarium is nature's church and a great urban builder of momentum and energy.

The process fascinated me. Trammell Crow, a development partner and board member, did some architectural drawings and helped get Tampa's mayor to put up a guarantee, which was critical to our financing. Then Trammell Crow had to pull out in 1991, and we were left without an architect or any drawings. We did have an exhibit plan through Joe Wetzel, and the head of Carrigan Development Company, an experienced builder and also a board member. So we decided to do a Request for Proposal.

Many people responded, including the fellow who designed the Baltimore and Boston aquariums, the person creating the Shedd Aquarium addition, and Chuck Davis from Escherick Homsey Dodge and Davis out of San Francisco, who designed the Monterey Bay Aquarium. Gyo Obata and HOK came in as strong architects with a local Tampa office. The head of their office, Pete Karamitsanis, knew a lot of the board members.

Gyo and HOK impressed the decision committee with their varied experiences in every part of the world;

LEFT Bright, festive colors in the Florida sun
RIGHT A controlled, indoor climate created by a domed-shaped greenhouse

however, they had never designed an aquarium. We also were very taken with Chuck Davis and his experience in Monterey. Someone said, "Wouldn't it be a miracle if these two hugely successful people could work together?" So, I was commissioned to go to California and talk with Chuck Davis. We liked the Monterey Bay Aquarium as the best aquarium design because it focused on exhibition rather than on architecture.

We chose the team partly because our architectural theory positioned the exhibits first. The job of the architect was not to make something beautiful from the outside in. This was to be captivating from the inside out. Imagine one of the most famous architects in the world being told that the client does not want anything that displaces the story inside, and that the architecture needs to flow from the exhibition story. That could pose a huge block to creative genius.

This project gave me an experience of leadership without power. At Harvard, we learned how to make good decisions allocating assets, but we were not taught what to do when we had no assets, only a wonderful dream. A powerful dream, translated into a clear project vision, can serve as a magnetic force attracting like-minded people to support the project.

I wrote a three-page memo which identified the two times in my life that an architectural presence transformed me: once in 1963 when I walked into Chartres Cathedral, and again when I visited the Monterey Bay Aquarium in 1985. I concluded that we can bring the sacred present and ground it in reality in such a way that the mind cannot trick us into thinking it is just another space. Something happens. There are qualities to the design and there are qualities behind the intention. I said, "Let's make it like these two places."

Linda Rose and Chuck Davis suggested that we hold a retreat to develop a coherent and shared vision of our goal. We took three days, and for two of those days Gyo sat for eight hours. Pete Karamitsanis from HOK joked, "You don't know how rare it is to have Gyo Obata sit in one space for two days."

It looked like we could only spend $39.4 million on construction, including fees. It also appeared that we were going to be way over that because the aquarium was too big given the design plan. I had a sinking feeling in my stomach; this could kill us before we really got started.

Then Chuck Davis stood up in the design charrette and led the charge saying, "Let's draw it." Those were the crucial words we needed.

At our next design review, we were happily told that the full exhibit story could be housed in a space we could

RIGHT Visitors are totally immersed in the large tank experience

afford to build. From that point until project completion, we stayed on or under the $39.4 million budget.

At one point, I sat down with Gyo. He pulled out a piece of paper that revealed he had been down on the beach with his wife, Courtney, and had been drawing shells. A few weeks later, elements of this beach-discovered shell appeared on the wall in the form of the huge glass shell roof. It was stunning. We never found that paper again, as it got lost in the process. I felt that piece of paper evidenced the design process of someone with great wisdom and experience, but also of someone with an open soul who will never grow old. He was like a kid on the beach with shells that suddenly became a roof. That roof is far and away the major architectural element of the Florida Aquarium.

Money was difficult. We had to shut down the project from the end of 1991 until mid-1992 because the city could not proceed with their guarantee, which was our only way of getting financing. The team went on to other jobs. We had an incredible honesty with each other. During a giant conference call across the country with the project architect and others, I was asked if I had any evidence that the project would go forward. I said, "No." Then they asked if I believed in my heart that it would go forward. I answered, "Absolutely." And across the multiple locations of the conference call, you could hear the words: "Well that's good enough for me."

From that moment on, people continued to work without billing, instead of disbanding their teams. About six months later, the mayor agreed to go forward with the city guarantee, and the financing materialized. In August 1992, we passed a bond issue. In mid-1993, we broke ground. In mid-1995, on schedule and ahead of budget, the Florida Aquarium opened its doors.

This project's high-performing team worked what Joseph Jaworski in his book *Synchronicity: The Inner Path of Leadership* would call "predictable miracles." We bounced back from the city saying "no" and from being thrown off our site. Determination and the power of creativity brought definitive events into place. It would have been very tempting for Gyo and HOK to say, "Let's write this stuff off and go on to something else." But they did not.

Everyone on this team contributed to the project. One day when we were designing the gigantic reef at the aquarium, a big design problem arose. We wanted the people to be immersed in the water environment as much as possible. Walt Eidam, a cost accountant for Turner Construction and a fisherman, made a critical suggestion that allowed the large tank exhibit to go forward. His voice was fully heard at the table and he helped solve one of our biggest challenges. Gyo is a powerful, creative person all by himself, but in this project he was wonderfully supportive.

It was a transformative project and a life-changing experience for me. It cemented my belief that the inner vitality of individuals and teams, the quality of commitment and sharing, and the ideas exchanged between one guy walking on the beach and another guy fishing can all be made visible.

The Florida Aquarium has given Tampa a beautiful, educational, and entertaining venue that helps people think about conservation and their role as stewards of the environment. It also has rejuvenated the empty and neglected waterfront area, which enhances and benefits Tampa. This energized area has become "the hot river walk," with everyone enjoying the space.

Jim Stuart served as the Founding Executive Director of the Florida Aquarium. He is a retired businessman.

FEDERAL RESERVE BANK OF MINNEAPOLIS

HEADQUARTERS AND OPERATIONS CENTER, MINNEAPOLIS, MINNESOTA

GYO OBATA: EXPRESSING AUTHORITY WITHOUT PRETENSION

The Federal Reserve had this wonderful site where the city of Minneapolis actually began, right on the banks of the Mississippi River. We needed to tie this project with the river and downtown Minneapolis.

We interviewed and were selected for this project. Gary Stern, the President of the district's Federal Reserve Bank, and his facility people were our clients. Our many meetings together were a great experience.

Federal Reserve operations have two sides. There's an industrial side, where checks, coins, and bills are brought in and sorted in an efficient, factory-like atmosphere. The office side provides work spaces for people who run the Federal Reserve, including the head of the district. Knowing this informed the building design.

I positioned the offices perpendicular to the river, giving the spaces on both sides of the floor views of the Mississippi. On the other side, I located the sections for the functional movement of coins, checks, and bills. I designed those areas so they could expand. Between them, I placed the dining and meeting areas.

This is a contemporary building. The offices have a lot of glass facing east, which brings in good light. The west side is not as glassy, so we installed punch windows because of the west sun. For the exterior, we used precast concrete and matched it to the color of Kasota stone. The site is at the end of the downtown, so we built a clock tower that faces the city. Along the Mississippi, the City of Minneapolis has a park space. We created an appealing landscaped area, a walking path to the river, and interpretives that tell the rich history of the locale.

The Federal Reserve represents the highest ideals of our government. Our building needed to communicate a level of importance and authority without being overly pretentious. We designed it to express confidence and trustworthiness, essential character elements of the Federal Reserve Bank.

I like to design buildings that are convenient and understandable for the people who use them. We took the requirements of the project and melded them with the community and the intended site. I believe that this building serves the Federal Reserve well.

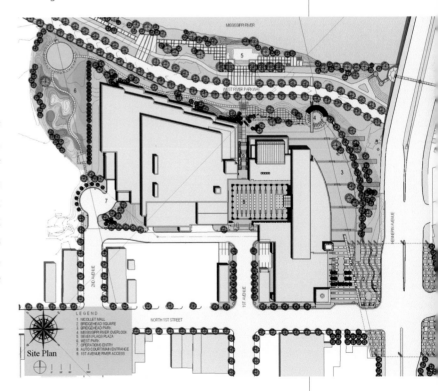

GARY STERN: MEETING THE CHALLENGE OF APPROVAL

To acquire a major piece of land in a major metropolitan area right on the Mississippi River is fairly unique. HOK designed a building that capitalized on that site location.

I am President of the Federal Reserve Bank of Minneapolis and was at the time of this project. We were occupying a building just a few buildings away from our current site in downtown Minneapolis. While it was considered architecturally distinctive, it had operational and structural problems. We conducted a thorough analysis as to whether the smart thing would be to fix the old building and continue to occupy it, or to move out, build a new building, and sell the old one. From a number of perspectives, selling the old one and building a new one was the financially sound decision to make. So that is what we did.

Choosing an architect required a fairly lengthy process. As I recall, it involved senior management of the Federal Reserve Bank, members of the Board of Directors, as well as Federal Reserve people from Washington. We conducted an elaborate search. We sent out a Request for Proposal to a number of architectural firms. The staff then did a preliminary review of the materials and ultimately narrowed the number down to three: one based in Minneapolis, one in St. Louis, and one in New York.

Senior management and some members of the Board of Directors interviewed all three firms in their offices. We did this back to back to back. We looked at their proposals, their understanding of the project, and the fees submitted. As you would expect, we asked, "What is it going to cost if we go with firm A as opposed to firms B or C?" We then made the decision to go with Obata.

Our decision was based on a combination of factors. We felt comfortable with the HOK people. We liked their additional thoughts on what we needed to do to get a new building that would do well and function efficiently. And their fees were competitive. These three factors were significant, but I remember that there were many other major considerations. The firm already had a good reputation within the Federal Reserve. They had done other work for the Fed and other Fed people thought highly of the firm because they understood our operational needs, our needs for security, and our budget constraints. All of those things were important.

RIGHT The park-like setting mixes sculpture, lighting, lawns, and walkways

At the time, we were looking at three separate plots of land downtown, and it was not clear which one we would wind up acquiring. HOK's initial proposal focused on a different site, but it was meant to be illustrative, not definitive. I thought the proposal was actually terrific, but the site was too small. Eventually, we wound up with this site and the building turned out to be quite different. That decision did not present any special problems for Gyo or for us.

The people here in the Federal Reserve wanted a building that functioned well, met the needs of our staff and operations, and was reliable in the sense that it was warm in the winter and cool in the summer. That was number one. Design and amenities and those things were number two. The previous building put the emphasis on architecture at the expense of practicality, functionality, and reliability. What we wound up getting was an operationally efficient and well-designed building. It is not only reliable and functional, but architecturally it takes wonderful advantage of the site. I think, in some sense, we got two for one out of this.

Throughout the project, Gyo seemed low-key and thoughtful. He was very open and responsive, and a good listener to our concerns, and not at all reserved about telling us what he thought. Maybe the best thing about it was that he would give his rationale. He would explain why he thought certain things should or should not be done. It wasn't so much, "Just trust me." He could explain the basis for whatever it was he was proposing or recommending. And, he put together a team and a plan that did a wonderful job of satisfying our requirements. Obviously, with his track record, he is a consummate professional in the field.

The most exciting part of the project for me will surprise you. It doesn't really have anything to do with Gyo. I was involved in another building project in the Federal Reserve in Helena, Montana, that HOK was not. A big stumbling block in building Federal Reserve buildings is getting approval from the Federal Reserve staff and officials in Washington. A lot of people are important in getting that approval, including the staff and directors in the region. And, if the architects have a good reputation, it goes better than if they do not. So the most exciting moment for me was when we got that approval. I say that because officials do not go out of their way to make it easy—and for good reason. I knew that once we had the approval, we would be able to get the project done. Until then, there was no telling what was going to happen.

BELOW The materials relate to nearby, historic buildings

Actually, the most difficult part was dealing with the City of Minneapolis. They had a master plan that had the property we are on devoted to residential development. We had to convince them that it made sense to put the Federal Reserve Bank here. That alone was a major undertaking. Then, when we acquired the land and were readying it for construction, we discovered historic artifacts buried beneath the surface.

The artifacts we unearthed were not bricks and mortar, but rather the remains of glassware, plates, parts of plates and such, that had been in the first buildings on this property during the second half of the 19th century. We were involved with the historical society, trying to recover and preserve the artifacts they considered important. All of this may sound trivial, but it turned out that it wasn't. It put a real burden on the staff because they went to countless meetings with city officials and preservationists, none of whom wanted to be particularly agreeable to all of this. And the staff had to keep the objective in mind that we wanted to build on this property.

Getting the approvals was the major challenge. It may simply be the cost of doing business in any metropolitan area. But it is a cost that imposes a lot on the staff and that is unfortunate. Once we got the approval from the city and Washington, things went smoothly. Even during the Minnesota winter, we continued construction unless it got really cold. I believe that the threshold is 10 degrees below zero or something like that. So, once we got underway, the project went very smoothly and it came in on time and on or under budget.

Our vision for the building was surpassed. We achieved operational efficiency and functionality along with wonderful architecture. The building has worked out better than anyone anticipated. It has been efficient and we have had no problems with it whatsoever. We have been here 12 years, so I think that is testimony in itself. And, as a place to go to work every day, it is as good as you are going to find in my judgment. I don't think it is the only nice place to work in Minneapolis or in this country, but it is certainly among the nicest.

Looking at this building, I would say that it recalls some aspects of the old, distinguished City Hall building that is about six or eight blocks away. We are right across the street from the major downtown post office, which I do not consider a distinguished piece of architecture. We wanted to make sure that we didn't have a building design that clashed, and that goal has been accomplished. The Hennepin Avenue Bridge, a small suspension bridge that goes over the Mississippi River, is directly next door. So, our Federal Reserve Bank building fits in the environment very well.

The building achieved our multiple objectives. It is operational, functional, and efficient, and architecturally appropriate. It is something that the people in the bank and the community like. I do not know what would have happened had we picked another architectural firm, but from what I can tell, we chose wisely. I take a measure of pride in the fact that this building was done during my tenure. I am obviously very pleased with it.

Gary Stern is the President of the Federal Reserve
Bank of Minneapolis.

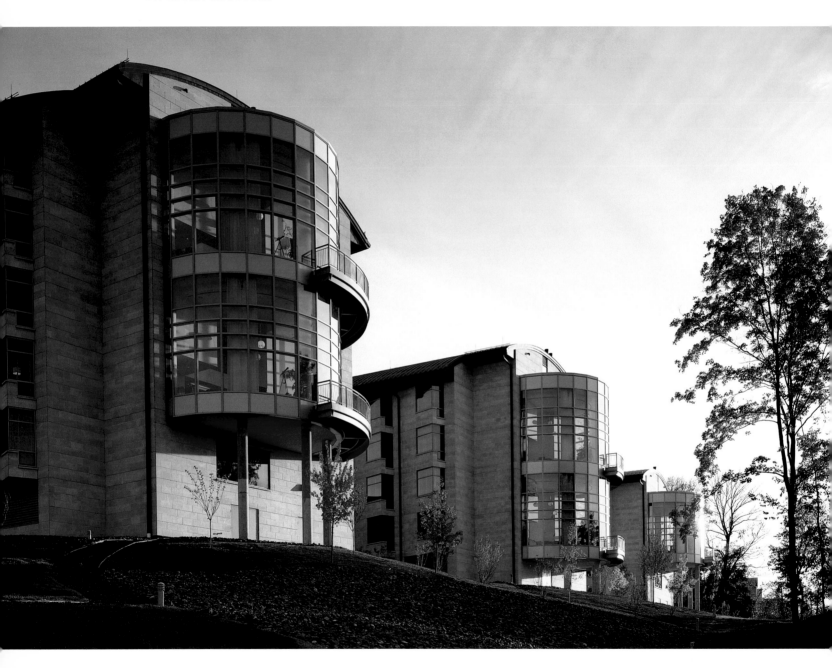

GYO OBATA: A RIVER OVERLOOK

In St. Louis, we have the two great rivers: the Mississippi and the Missouri. Yet so few of our buildings relate to the rivers. I think it is important to design buildings that acknowledge and maximize views of these waterways, and make them part of our daily life.

McDonnell Douglas, now The Boeing Company, purchased a beautiful property on the bluffs of the Missouri River that at one time belonged to the Desloge family of St. Louis. The company held a competition with two other firms and HOK to see who would be selected to create a new center for conferences and education. Harry Stonecipher, the Chief Executive Officer, said, "When McDonnell Douglas goes after a job, we always compete." He wanted the architects to do the same. They liked the scheme HOK presented. Conference expert Frank Bordonaro, then Chief Learning Officer of the Company, directed the project. Shortly thereafter, McDonnell Douglas merged with Boeing. Because the cultures of the two companies were quite different, the project provided an ideal way to bring Boeing's top leaders to St. Louis for conferences.

I assessed the site and found that it included an estate with an allée of trees leading to a view of the Missouri River bluffs. I did not want to disturb a famous family ballroom where many St. Louis people frequently attended social galas. In times past, ladies dressed in their most expensive gowns and finery would arrive at the carriage entrance and walk down a long, underground walkway to the ballroom. Those were memories too rich to disturb.

The two primary issues for HOK revolved around the movement of people within the space and the relationship to the site. We employed the concept of a spine, with people moving along a "central nervous system" corridor with hotel rooms and a dining area that overlooked the bluffs and the river. In addition, we created a conference center with lecture halls, meeting rooms, and breakout rooms for instruction and discussion. We slanted all the windows so that everyone had a view of the Missouri. Outside, we created walkways where people could jog or hike into the woods to the river. The old ballroom was preserved for meetings.

I enjoyed helping McDonnell Douglas and Boeing create a conference and education center. The site is dramatic. The river views inspired the overall design.

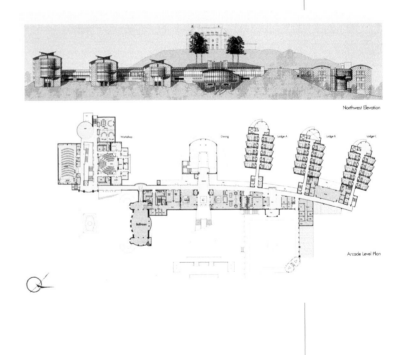

FRANK BORDONARO: AN INSPIRATIONAL LEARNING SPACE

The human dynamics of learning and work became the guiding principles for the architect. From the beginning, we had the cart and the horse in the right positions.

I served as the Chief Learning Officer of McDonnell Douglas and held that title throughout my time there. My tenure preceded the Boeing merger, so the original project was done as a McDonnell Douglas project. Harry Stonecipher was the original executive sponsor. He and Phil Condit, Chairman and CEO of Boeing, jointly supported and sponsored the project.

McDonnell Douglas, under Harry Stonecipher, was concerned about the supply of talent from within the company. They had not found a way to develop the next generation of executives. Harry would say that neither he nor I should be there because the company should have been able to grow leaders internally. He felt that stronger response people were needed to prepare the next generation of company leadership. We crafted a mission statement: the purpose of the learning center was to make McDonnell Douglas more valuable by growing the capacity of its people to learn, to work together, and to lead. We thought that defined our purpose.

As the officer in charge, I managed the project. We had selected some land and were in the middle of negotiations for the purchase when I joined the company. My job was to choose the architect and builder, manage the design and building construction, and develop a leadership curriculum for the new center. I held an architectural competition with three architectural firms. HOK won because of how it integrated site and design.

The site consisted of 167 acres in Florissant. The mansion on the property occupied the ideal site, which left us with a number of options as to how to best use the place. Gyo and I discussed what to do. He remarked that the best site was on top of the hill. I went to Harry and suggested we tear down the mansion. He almost came out of his chair, and never let me forget it. So, our task became how we would create a really compelling experience.

HOK embraced an aggressive and creative use of the site, taking advantage of the dramatic drop-off and views. The building's footprint faces the confluence of the Missouri and Mississippi Rivers. It is a magical place in a way. The summer sun sets beyond the glass expanses, as if on cue. We knew about the uniqueness of that site because the

original ballroom was built with that in mind. We used it to our advantage.

During our second meeting together, Gyo turned to me and asked a simple question, "As an industrial psychologist and expert in these things, how do you think people make decisions?" I took that question home with me and drew a series of cartoons showing how individuals and clusters of various-sized groups gather in order to make decisions. I sent them to Gyo and a couple of days later, he stopped by my office.

When we met, he unrolled a sheath of papers to reveal a series of drawings featuring clusters of rooms sharing a common space. He did some quick pencil work to show how that configuration could be multiplied three times for the stories of the building and four times across, resulting in the total room count for the program. Gyo had transformed decision dynamics into an organizing theme for the project.

I thought that was wonderful, and it forged an immediate connection between Gyo and me. I realized we would be building a unique structure designed around how people work. I credit him for the original design where

form followed function in the classic sense, but also in a new, creative way. I knew of no other learning centers built that way.

The building evolved over time and there were changes. When we merged with The Boeing Company and needed more space than originally expected, we lengthened the hallways, increased the number of rooms, modified the learning space, and focused on creating groups of rooms where people could even have their own rooms if they stayed for a length of time. There would also be a common space with a fireplace, library, and a General Electric-inspired kitchenette. GE discovered that momentous conversations and decisions occur in kitchens where people gather.

Gyo and his team were so good at listening and compiling the best wisdom. We arranged a meeting with Harry Stonecipher, Gyo, Ram Charan (the management guru), and me. Ram wrote a book with Larry Bossidy and Charles Burck titled *Execution: The Discipline of Getting Things Done*. The four of us had breakfast together and talked about the learning needs of the organization.

Ram and Gyo traded ideas as well. Gyo and I asked Ram what the best learning space was he had ever used. He identified Room 109 in Aldrich Hall at Harvard Business School. Gyo and his team found that very room, got the drawings from Harvard, and replicated it to the square inch. Ram claimed the pitch and space of the aisles, and the number and configuration of seats were ideal for teaching. That room became the heart of the learning spaces.

Because the project was going to take two years, we looked closely at the carriage house as a key to our success. It was a 6,000-square-foot, open-ceiling building designed in the French chateau style to match the mansion. We gave

The first job of any team that came in was to create their own workspace. They could establish Internet connections, roll a white board from one side to another, put up a partition for privacy, clip together a table, and choose chairs best suited for their work. The carriage house became a point of excitement for the company, as well as a laboratory to help us understand how best to equip and use the new space. After the Boeing merger, we held the very first joint Board of Directors meeting there, which fueled their interest in the learning center.

We ended up with an inspirational learning space that communicates to people that innovation is a big part of leadership. The bold envelope itself is an innovation. It inspires learning and provides for individual reflection in rooms with gorgeous river views. Two people can walk around the grounds and talk; three people can meet in small enclaves; and four or five people can work in breakout rooms and in numerous "found spaces." The resident groups live in clusters and use the libraries to socialize, deliberate, and produce work. The environment also fosters spontaneous interaction and new connections within the company. Groups come together in common spaces, and individuals regularly "run into" valuable contacts along the spinal corridor. In short, the design facilitates the company's mission of growing the capacity of its people to learn, work together, and lead.

it a $3.5 million makeover that simulated the environment we wanted. We also made it a laboratory with a huge, open space, and a balcony where people could observe from above the patterns of interaction. We asked the furniture companies to supply their best new chairs and furniture. Chairs were on rollers, and tables were modular and could be taken apart, reconfigured, and reassembled. We watched how people used the space.

Gyo is an unassuming person with a great amount of knowledge and understanding. He has a quiet depth, and is a wonderful listener. The question he asked me about decision-making was crucial. Without it, that building would be something very different today. He knew that boldness and innovation were essential. He made it possible for us to create the laboratory in the carriage house, so we could

try out new ideas. He sat in on our classes and participated. This is a brilliant example of how a person who listens can influence the entire shape of a project.

I am a psychologist by training, have taught at a university, and eventually went corporate. This project was a jump in scope and complexity for me. Not many psychologists have control of that much capital and that many people dependent on their leadership. It made me a better decision maker because anyone who has ever renovated a house knows that there are hundreds of decisions involved and no time to defer them.

Through Gyo's example, I am also a better listener. He gives people space to experiment with their own thinking and listens carefully to their preferences and their conclusions. He did that with me. He paid attention to my answers and conclusions. The happiest day of this whole ordeal was when we finally opened the first session and the carriage house was filled with people. I think it brought me a greater appreciation of how individuals learn. It made me less conceptual and more emotionally engaged in the power of learning.

To me, the building suggests preparation for flight. It is perched on a bluff and looks out over the tops of trees with the whole world before it. We are ready to take off and do something new. From the learners' views, the building recedes and what remains is the world outside. In their preparation for flight, they are poised and ready on the runway.

Exciting!

Frank P. Bordonaro, Ph.D., was the Chief Learning Officer for McDonnell Douglas, now Boeing, in St. Louis, Missouri, and later served in the same role for Prudential Financial. Today, he works on digital learning applications and architectural projects that support learning and innovation.

BRISTOL-MYERS SQUIBB COMPANY

LAWRENCEVILLE, NEW JERSEY

GYO OBATA: COMPLEMENTING THE NATURAL LOCATION

The building is placed in natural surroundings, set back from the main road to relate to the neighborhood. The lake and trees create a park-like environment.

E.R. Squibb & Sons chose a beautiful site near Princeton, New Jersey, on which to build their corporate headquarters and their main research laboratories. Squibb worried that people might be concerned about having a large corporate campus in this location. They hired a special consultant to select the architect and manage the project. HOK was awarded the project.

Visually, the architecture was simple: limestone on a concrete structure with brick and glass. A small stream ran along the front of the property. In the design, we added a dam and a big lake in the foreground. We set the building back and hid the parking between two tree lines. From the roadway, passersby could see the lake with the building in the background. The community approved the project.

To promote employee satisfaction, we designed a nature-oriented environment. The dining room was set slightly in-ground, next to the lake. People dine seated at water level. From the dining area, the building's spine extends all the way to the back of the property. Next to the spine, we designed an atrium with skylights. Along the spine, office units and laboratories branch out, and lounge areas let scientists meet and talk. Continued growth occurs.

The lake, although beautiful, attracted migrating geese. A tiny and barely visible metal fence was installed along the water's edge to keep the birds from entering the water. Ultimately, it discouraged their visits to that serene setting.

Proper site orientation, movement, light, and landscaping are key design elements. An architectural goal is to create an environment that benefits and facilitates the activity on the premises. Movement informs design: how the people flow from their cars into the building and then move about within the building. Light is everywhere. The offices and research laboratories have windows that admit natural light into the workspace.

As I reflect on this project, I realize it was about discovery. I wanted to design an inspiring place. In this building, people can meet, mix, and create.

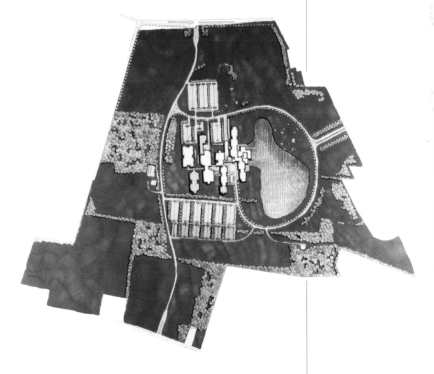

LEFT The low complex is composed of clustered buildings off a central spine

143

DESIGN THAT EXPRESSES VALUES

Perhaps I am biased, but to me Bristol-Myers Squibb's Lawrenceville campus is one of the most pleasant workplace settings in New Jersey.

The building's design excels in terms of form and function. It is also a statement of key corporate principles. The integration of these qualities is its hallmark.

As for form, the park-like setting and clean, simple building design convey an understated elegance. Though the campus dates to the 1970s, its style isn't easily pinpointed to that decade, or any other period. It has a more classic quality. When you drive by, it looks like a modern and elegant corporate building fitting naturally in its surroundings.

The expansive, open spaces around the buildings help to convey a sense of serenity. If you have been here, you understand the peaceful feeling offered by looking out from office windows toward our lake or the snow-covered fields. The outdoor environment is enhanced by many well-tended and mature trees, carefully manicured shrubs, hedges, and groundcover, and several landscaped courtyards.

Indoors, our common areas are also pleasant and elegant. A three-story atrium near the main entrance is filled with natural light from skylights and two-story windows. A range of materials including slate, marble, wood, glass, and brick adds to the visual appeal. There are numerous planters and even a small waterfall.

While our campus is aesthetically pleasing, it also is functional and efficient. It serves as a corporate building and fulfills a serious and complex research function.

The overall building layout is open and modular. The many buildings, or modules, are interconnected like branches along a central spine. Office areas and laboratories are all

LEFT Abundant, natural light brightens the central spine and corridors
RIGHT A tranquil, park-like setting welcomes employees and visitors

linked. Tall windows let in the light virtually everywhere you go. There also are many seating areas for impromptu meetings. The campus has been expanded throughout the years using the plan in place at the beginning. As large as our complex is, the working spaces are more intimate, so you don't get the sense you are in a vast place.

Finally, the design of our campus also makes a statement of corporate values. As home to both research laboratories and our global business divisions, the Lawrenceville site brings together people across many disciplines, from science and engineering to finance, marketing, and other professions. This environment fosters a shared sense of mission and a common corporate culture around the values of excellence, leadership, and innovation.

Whether you spend most of your day in the laboratories or in the executive offices, we all work together and enjoy lunch together. We understand we are part of a business and part of a scientific community. We are united in the same enterprise: helping patients prevail over serious diseases.

Bristol-Myers Squibb's Vice President of Facilities Operations for Wallingford and Central New Jersey contributed to this section.

IN HARMONY WITH THE ENVIRONMENT

Bristol-Myers Squibb prides itself on being a good neighbor wherever our facilities are located, and the successful design of our Lawrenceville campus helps set a positive tone in our relations with the community.

Set back from the road, buffered from residential neighbors by woods and open space, this large facility is not out of place in an area that values open space and strives to preserve its rural heritage. We have a strong relationship with the surrounding Princeton/Lawrenceville community, and through the years our campus has come to be part of its fabric. Each morning, you see people jogging, cycling, walking their dogs, even bird-watching. The campus also hosts numerous community events, from small art exhibits in our gallery to major gatherings, such as the Race for the Cure walk for cancer and the Tour de Cure bicycle ride.

The buildings themselves are very welcoming. They have multiple stories, but are not imposing because of the way they naturally meld into the landscape. There is a comfortable feel to our campus—a nice cross between an academic environment and a business environment—much different from a typical plant or office facility. Our scientific community appreciates the academic flavor.

Our employees also appreciate the campus's natural setting. The facility has earned certification from the Wildlife Habitat Council for the efforts employees have made protecting and restoring wildlife habitat. The initiatives include a nesting box program to increase the number of native bird species, and a native plant restoration effort that has added some 3,000 herbaceous plants at the edge of our lake.

Bristol-Myers Squibb's Director of Community Affairs contributed information for this section.

148

GYO OBATA: PAST AND FUTURE CONNECT IN THE PRESENT

I really believe in the Zen concept about being in the present moment. I never look back, you know. Forward always! When I do return to projects I have designed and find that they are working well, it gives me pleasure.

The board members of the Japanese American National Museum (JANM) wanted to create a cultural center documenting Japanese immigration and acculturation to America. They wanted to record forever the incarceration of 120,000 Japanese Americans—my family included—from West Coast cities during World War II. When I was invited to design this project, I readily accepted the opportunity.

Irene Hirano, the Director of the JANM, almost single-handedly brought this project to fruition. The museum originally inhabited an old Buddhist temple. The new site was located across the street at the corner of First Street and Central Avenue in the Little Tokyo Historic District of downtown Los Angeles.

Using an image of connecting curves, I tried to express the design idea of two cultures coming together at a common meeting point. The museum features an outdoor pavilion, an open reception area, and galleries on two levels that house the legacy of Japanese Americans, including the Issei, the first generation like my father and mother. The intention is to keep traditions alive and help younger generations understand their heritage.

I created a Japanese garden with Robert Murase, a landscape architect and third-generation Japanese American. Using a curvilinear motif, we formed a small, meditative garden with falling water, and placed a small restaurant at the end. The garden masks the city noise and evokes tranquility.

Between the old Buddhist temple and the new building we set a plaza. The museum hosts many outdoor activities there. In 1999, the museum opening was held in the courtyard between the old and new buildings. A Shinto priest shot his arrow and hit the bull's-eye of a big target. With that, the facade of the building erupted in bright, colored streamers. It was fantastic!

Originally, the museum was created to document the internment of the Japanese American people. Now it showcases art and culture, and has hosted exhibits of Noguchi and Asawa. This was an inspiring project for me to work on because it celebrates my family's legacy.

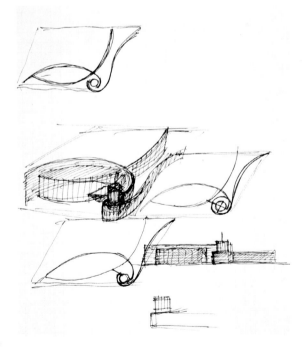

IRENE Y. HIRANO: WHERE EAST AND WEST COME TOGETHER

Our building houses legacy in wonderful ways. It tells the legacy through stories that inspire others to think about what those stories mean in their own lives.

When the museum's original founders were creating their vision and plans, they asked a select few individuals for advice. One of those people was Gyo Obata. The museum had procured its original building, a former Buddhist temple, located across the plaza. While it was a wonderful building to begin this story, it is not a museum building.

Gyo was among those who provided the board with a broad vision. He said, "If you are going to create an institution, it needs to provide a permanent legacy and a home for the collection that you want to create." So when we began work on the original historic building, we knew it was the precursor for actual museum space. While we restored a former Buddhist temple, we did not create a museum. The master plan called for a second plan that would create a state-of-the-art museum facility to house collections and exhibition galleries and to provide public spaces worthy of a national museum.

The board wanted Gyo to design the second building. He had reputation and experience as an architect, plus his personal history reflected the Japanese American experience. He was destined to help fulfill the JANM vision.

We knew we wanted a state-of-the-art museum. The original design called for the expansion pavilion to be behind the historic building. Then, through a series of serendipitous events, the city had a master plan for this neighborhood. We changed mayors and the plans changed. We had a very good friend in the newly elected mayor's office, and through persuasion and persistence, we were able to get this parcel. So, the land belongs to the city; it is on long-term lease. The plaza, this land, and the original historic building are all part of city property. We have a 55-year lease on this facility.

I hoped to build a building that would facilitate the kind of programming and exhibitions we knew we could take to a larger audience. We sat down with Gyo and HOK and talked about the museum's vision and mission, what we wanted the building to house, what we hoped to create, what had already been done, and our perceived direction.

LEFT The facade is captivating, open, and welcoming

Many conversations concerned the institution. While Gyo had been involved in early conversations with the board, much had developed over time.

After these great conversations, Gyo's staff worked with our staff to map out our building requirements in concert with the board's vision. When we began to see on paper how this was going to unfold, it took many months of focused thought about what the most important elements were to include.

We were concerned about the original historic building becoming a stepchild. We wanted Gyo and HOK to help us create a campus in Little Tokyo where we would bring together the old, the new, and the future. We wanted to talk about the historic building, its early role in the museum's history and its relationship to the new facility. Consequently, the museum's main hall looks out onto the historic building. It was a brilliant way to acknowledge the historic building, while at the same time creating the connection with the new building and the future.

We also talked about the philosophy of the East and West and the historic challenges of that relationship. We knew in the future that the museum was going to be that place for the East and West to come together. We wanted to create a space that would fully explore that relationship. Aerial views show two circles coming together and meeting in the corner. When Gyo was designing the building, we spent a lot of time on the corner space. While there were a number of opinions, we finally agreed on an optimal solution and all became good friends.

Gyo's design reflects that East and West connection, which is symbolic of who we are as an institution, but more importantly, where we know we are going in the

future. And while we were not yet there, the aspiration of eventually being able to do that was another important aspect of the building.

A third challenge we faced was an intangible aesthetic about what is Japanese American design—what features reflect the Japanese American experience. People are familiar with Japanese architecture or design, and historically there have been many Japanese American artists, designers, and architects. We wanted the building to express that culture and aesthetic. It is very intangible. So, as the design evolved, the building materials specified for the interior space included wood, stone, and glass to let people know they were walking into a Japanese American environment. When Japanese Americans come

153

in, they feel right at home in the space. This is a difficult aesthetic to capture and yet I think the building does it wonderfully well.

The people love the building and have since the day we opened in 1999. When we survey visitors and members, we ask them what they like about the institution. At the top of the list comes, "Oh, we love the building." That is what Gyo has given us. This project was never about him or his design or his signature, but about creating a space for our exhibitions, programs, gatherings, and collections. Photographs, oral histories, and diaries are housed in the middle of the building, symbolizing the heart of the institution.

Museum buildings mostly become the signature buildings of the signature architects who design them. That was not Gyo's approach. This was very much our building. He said we were the client and that HOK was working for us. He brought his own personal experience and aesthetic to the project, and built the team that fulfilled it. The process was collaborative and inclusive. Gyo listened to what we said we wanted. Within the building, we wanted the flexibility to create spaces that could be used in a variety of ways in the future. We did not feel it was right to lock down on specific design elements. That proved to be a good choice.

I love when this building is filled with school children. There is such a buzz. And yet they are looking at very serious stories about history. We see students of Hispanic, African American, and Japanese backgrounds engaged by the volunteers, learning and understanding a very difficult chapter in our history. World War II is ancient history to

most young people and so I really appreciate whenever I see the building filled with young people. The building's design enables that story to be told in an environment that almost contradicts the seriousness of the story. And yet it is very fitting that it exudes warmth to people as they walk through the spaces. I am pleased that the building feels so vibrant and alive.

Little Tokyo is changing rapidly. There is new housing being developed and a new subway line being built right across the street. One always worries about the future of an institution's neighborhood. It is encouraging to see the growth around us. We have to believe that the success of the museum has helped attract others to downtown Los Angeles. We finished an addition to our regular historic building a couple of years ago—a 200-seat forum. We created a new Center for the Preservation of Democracy.

So we need to make sure that this building continues to do all the things we want it to do. This is part of our ongoing and future work.

I most appreciate having had the opportunity to meet and work with so many talented people. Working with Gyo was wonderful. I have gotten to know his family and to learn about his parents and others in the Obata family. There is a real legacy there. Like so many others in the Japanese American community who were significantly affected by World War II, they could have been very bitter about the hardships they had to go through and what the war cost their families. Yet they were determined that when the war was over, they would rebuild their lives. They were going to make it better for their children, who went on to do remarkable things. The stories are wonderful and inspiring. We wish we had the time and resources to gather these stories faster.

Gyo is an accomplished American architect. His Japanese ancestry becomes a story about him, but the significant role that HOK has played in the field of architecture, and the many buildings they have done is a remarkable story. I think that what makes Gyo and the firm unique is the way they approach their work, focusing on the client relationship and the project outcome. That intangible quality of understanding our need and translating that into a design, into an aesthetic, into something that worked for our organization was critical to the success of this project. Gyo helped us create a significant legacy in the Japanese American National Museum, a legacy which is at once our own and America's as well.

Irene Y. Hirano was President and Chief Executive Officer of the Japanese American National Museum from 1988 to 2008.

GYO OBATA: A COMPLEMENTARY POLARITY

The word that describes my feeling about this project is "contrast." It posed the interesting challenge of juxtaposing a contemporary building with a classical building. I emphasized to the Trustees that they were building for the next century.

The museum, located at the northern entrance to Forest Park, was an entry point into the 1904 World's Fair. The site was very tight. An underground addition was built to avoid competing with the classical architecture, but it was unsuccessful.

Before my interview, I studied the site. I wanted the job, but only if the Board was open to a contemporary design. During the interview, I made some sketches separating the old building from the new building facing south overlooking the park. Museum Director Bob Archibald and the Board were intrigued. I got the job.

Requirements included exhibit space, an auditorium, a bookstore, a restaurant, and classrooms. Adjacent to the existing building, I put a glass passageway and two wings of the new exhibit halls on two levels. Next to that, I designed a very glassy contemporary building that faces Forest Park on the south. I placed the bookstore on the ground level and the restaurant on the second level, where people can enjoy views of the park while dining.

The exhibit hall and other new facilities had to be very contemporary. We created an open, expansive area at the entry. We also designed an acoustically excellent auditorium. It was an opportunity to be very open and inviting, to make a south entrance, and to let people face Forest Park. Despite the restrictive roundabout, we fit everything in, including the parking.

Bob Archibald wanted to bring the museum into the 21st century, with greater relevance to St. Louis's cultural mix. A courtyard and a garden ease the transition between the old and the new. In the central space between the old building and the new, my wife, Courtney, created a tile floor mosaic that acknowledges St. Louis as a river city. That central space became a favorite site for weddings, community activities, and celebrations. When you create a good space, people want to be in it and use it.

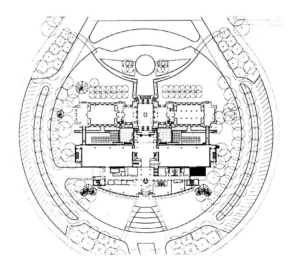

BOB ARCHIBALD: EDIFICE AS NARRATIVE

Everything is narrative. A story. We connect these stories together to make sense of our lives. And buildings are perhaps our most physical, pervasive, visible narrative. Buildings and the communities they inhabit tell us what we hope for the future.

The addition to the Missouri History Museum was designed to physically represent our values. We wanted the new building to reach out to the community, and to be accessible and sustainable. We wanted the building to say, "People belong here. You belong here. This is your building." History is a narrative about people.

The Missouri History Museum had been housed in the Jefferson Memorial Building since the early 1900s, and it was bulging at the seams with almost no exhibition space. In 1990–1991, we bought the former United Hebrew Temple and moved our collections and research space there. Once done, we turned our attention back to the Jefferson Memorial Building. We needed more exhibition

space to make more of our collections available to larger audiences and to have places for ancillary programming. That was the genesis of our thinking about this building.

From the time that I arrived here in late 1988, I knew we needed more visitors and more public space. There were a number of hurdles. We needed to build the institution's base in order to raise the necessary money. And Forest Park itself was very contested ground. We went through a long process to elevate the visibility, credibility, and fundraising potential of the institution, and to work with the Forest Park Master Plan.

We held conversations with Ted Wofford, the architect on the United Hebrew Temple. And we talked with John Hilberry, a museum design consultant from Michigan. We struggled with how to solicit proposals from and interview architects. So we engaged Professor Osmund Overby from the University of Missouri to discuss how to add to a historic Beaux Arts building constructed from materials that would be prohibitively expensive to replicate. There were a lot of ideas and we wanted to build something compatible with the existing structure. Osmund eventually brought us to the conclusion that if you have a good, old building, the best thing to do is build a good, new building.

Gyo came in and made the presentation on behalf of HOK. Our board and staff deliberated for some time, interviewed several firms, and finally chose Gyo based on his presentation. Gyo seemed to understand the possibilities of the site. He believed we could respect the old building while also creating something new. His vision was not a jarring

LEFT The design is a lively dialogue between existing and new buildings

contrast because it echoed some of the massing. He made us see all the possibilities, through his words and pictures.

When I first saw the design, I liked it. But I had to think always about functionality, public perception, and board reaction. I looked at it and thought it would work and that other people would like it too. It respected the Jefferson Memorial Building, preserving its architectural integrity. Also, I liked that if you went east or west of the building and looked at the sides, you saw the addition. It repeated the massing of the older building without replicating it. This makes it look like a cohesive part as opposed to a piece of modern architecture stuck on like an afterthought.

We were concerned about environmental sustainability, and wanted to set an example of being conservators of the environment. We brought in a German engineering firm that offered some assistance. This was prior to the U.S. Green Building Council's LEED (Leadership in Energy and Environmental Design) process. There were no guidelines for green buildings. One of our goals was to have updated mechanical systems in the buildings. The challenge to HOK and the engineering firm was to have both buildings consume less energy than the Jefferson Memorial Building consumed. Our building met the most advanced standards of our time. It was exciting.

Another aspect of the building is the significant role Courtney Obata played in designing and executing our floor mosaic. On the floor, in the central space, is an abstract design of the meeting of the great rivers in Missouri, created by Courtney. The mosaic incorporates many kinds of stone; some are smooth, shiny, and slick. It has never ceased to be a conversation piece, and even though it is stylized, everyone knows it is the river.

Our desire to create a museum filled with light, and open to the community and the park was a contradiction in terms. Museums are, by necessity, dark and closed-off spaces that protect artifacts and promote exhibit experiences. This building has done it all—it is both dark and light. Amazing. This building is a grand compliment to its creator, Gyo.

Gyo is obviously tops in his profession and has been for a long time. He is soft-spoken, but possesses a quiet strength. When you speak softly, other people must listen more carefully. Gyo is a master of that. His ideas were always exciting. Whenever he met with our board, his passion for the work came through his voice, despite his low-key manner. It was fun to watch someone who loves what he does. His passion for architecture and his belief in his ability have put him on top. And still he remains accessible.

There were many exciting aspects to this project. I had the thrill of knowing people will put money behind an idea or dream so that it manifests. I had the opportunity to learn about the collaborative process of designing and constructing buildings, and watching plans on paper become reality. And I had the gift of witnessing the favorable public reaction to what we created.

The difficult part was always budget. People have all kinds of expectations when a building is coming together. You begin initially with a huge menu of what people want. There is then an excruciating process of reverse prioritization when things have to come off the table, and sometimes they are things that people like a lot. That is not easy.

ABOVE The interplay of old and new architecture
LEFT Light and openness allow visitor circulation between levels

Creating a dream requires a commitment to values. We were very committed to including minority- and women-owned businesses in the construction process. We came to understand the challenges faced by minority- and women-owned businesses. In a project this size, there are huge bonding requirements that you are invoiced to pay every month. Small businesses have a hard time getting bonded. They have payroll to make and if they have to put out tens of thousands of dollars to purchase materials and do not get reimbursed for a month, that impacts their cash flow. So, we divided the project up into smaller jobs, so that small businesses could participate without bankrupting themselves. We lowered the bonding requirement because the jobs were small. We agreed to pay for the materials when they were delivered to the site, and to make payroll every two weeks instead of monthly. As a result, this building had close to 40 percent participation by minority contractors. I felt really good about that.

This project was a community effort. Hundreds and hundreds of people made it happen. I am grateful to all of them. I also have a lot of respect for this institution that has been here since 1866. Different people have been responsible for it at different times. I just happen to be the steward for this generation. But that does not mean I can undo the work of those who went before me. Instead, I can build on that legacy with my own generation. I am proud of our accomplishments and am humbled by the longevity of this institution and our place as temporary trustees. Others will pick up where we leave off. I hope we've built a timeless and enduring building.

Architecture is important. In our fast-paced world we may think of architecture as a framework within which we do something else. We minimize expenditure on buildings and their beautification, thinking it does not contribute to our bottom line. And so we end up with nondescript, cookie-cutter residential and commercial architecture.

If you drive through the older parts of the city, you find pedestrian streetscapes where people walk and meet, and buildings that have delivered form and function for many years. Beautiful places uplift people, enable them to feel connected to their surroundings, and garner commitment to maintaining that atmosphere for the future.

Gyo has designed a lot of buildings that fit this model —that make statements about beauty, strength, and longevity. The Missouri History Museum was designed to make everyone feel comfortable. It is a community place, where people meet, celebrate, and learn. With the glass transparency of the new addition, you see people moving around in the building. You view it as a people space. History is about people and our building is a great place for everyone.

Robert Archibald, Ph.D., is President of the Missouri History Museum.

RIGHT The center court's mosaic floor pattern mimics Missouri's rivers

GYO OBATA: CELEBRATING DEMOCRACY IN ARCHITECTURE

A courthouse is important to a democracy, and to design such a structure is an honor. Creating a building named after Tom Eagleton inspired me. And it was the tremendous support of all the judges that made it possible.

The General Service Administration (GSA) has built a number of courthouses all over the country and this was one of its projects. The St. Louis courthouse project sits on a very tight site. The building needed to contain several courts and called for a high-rise. Every building has challenges: the physical requirements and the movement of people. Architecture is all about solving problems.

Early in the design process, we met with Judge Edward Filippine and others to ask them how they wanted the building to feel. They clearly stated they wanted the courtrooms to feel dignified, and the building to reflect a democracy at work so that citizens would respect the space. We did a study of St. Louis City and made a lot of drawings.

We tried to infuse those aesthetics into the building with a high lobby and vertical columns. We could not afford stone, so we used precast concrete, which looks like stone. Security became a vital requirement, after the 1995 bombing in Oklahoma City. We carefully examined all security, which included protecting the building from a vehicle bomb, providing secure underground parking for judges, and installing special elevators.

The courthouse has an intricate system for moving people, prisoners, and judges to and within the courthouse and courtrooms. We organized all aspects, including an elaborate elevator system serving the entire building. Our design featured two-story courtrooms staggered on each side. And given the secure, high-rise nature of the building, we were able to admit daylight into the courtrooms. In

addition, each judge's one-story chamber is at the end of the same level as his or her courtroom. The courtrooms have views out to the city.

We were asked to relate the courthouse design to some of the area's traditional buildings, so we placed a stainless-steel dome on top to reference the Arch. Eero Saarinen, the designer of the Arch, asked that surrounding buildings be no more than 20 stories tall. The former Boatmen's Bank and Equitable buildings are about that height. A city cannot stop building high-rises.

LEFT The grand entrance inspires reverence for the justice system

167

EDWARD L. FILIPPINE: ORDER AND MAJESTY IN THE COURT

I was a little concerned about the location, but Gyo had a firm conviction that if we did it right,

we would create a new south front door to downtown.

In our court, we had a Space and Facilities Committee to address people's needs. This committee had a difficult job because we were jammed in our old courthouse on Market Street. About a year before I succeeded Judge Jack Nangle as chief, he told me that space and facilities were a big part of the chief's job and asked me to take over that committee.

We were trying to find ways to live inside our courthouse. We began working on surveys with Christner Partnership of St. Louis to see what improvements we could make in our building. In March 1990, Christner told the General Services Administration (GSA) that we had to expand in some way.

The question then became whether to annex or to build new. Being inexperienced in building, I thought we should annex it, but was told that it would be a big patchwork by Steinman, Grason, Smiley of Los Angeles, who did a spatial study. They suggested we needed a new courthouse. We then began looking for an architect.

The architect was actually chosen by the GSA, which owns almost all the government buildings. I wanted the court to have more say in the architect's selection. So four of us, the chief architects of the Administrative Office and the Eighth Circuit, our District Clerk and myself, flew to Kansas City, where the GSA gave us the documents that we spent a day reviewing in detail. We gave them our summary report and went home. When GSA was finished looking over the applications, they also selected Gyo's firm. We approved.

LEFT Natural light in the soaring atrium is suffused, reflected, and refracted
RIGHT A covered entrance with columns and a stainless-steel covered dome

HOK was chosen because of its experience, ability, imagination, and an impeccable work history. We were going to build a big courthouse and did not know exactly what it would look like. We needed someone we could work with and who was accessible.

When we met with Gyo the first time, he told us all about designing. He then asked me, "Judge, what do you want this courthouse to look like?" I told him that if two strangers were walking down the street, saw the building, and wondered what it was, I would want one to say to the other, "I don't know, but it looks like a courthouse."

Some people suggested we move out to Clayton, where we wouldn't have to pay earnings tax. Others suggested Jefferson Avenue. We wanted to stay downtown. The State Courts are here and most of the lawyers are in-house down near the courthouse.

Our lot was south of Market Street. At that time, anything south of Market was in an underdeveloped part of downtown. It wasn't considered a location for a nice building. North of Market, only small lots were available. But to the south we could get two large parking lots. Gyo told me, "Judge, if we do it right, we will create a new south front door to downtown." And that is exactly what we have done.

To the west of the courthouse is a hotel. Nearby, to the east, the Cupples Station warehouses were being refurbished as the Westin Hotel. Richard Baron, who was very much involved with that project, said publicly that had it not been for the new courthouse, they could never have received financing to refurbish the Cupples buildings and put the hotel there. Now there are all kinds of development plans, including putting a green belt to the south of us. We opened the door. Gyo was right.

Gyo is brilliant and knows his profession well. He listens intently, and when you are done speaking, he does not simply agree. Nor does he challenge your knowledge. He discusses pros and cons, and holds a real conversation. He never interrupts. It is a real art. Gyo was easy to work with, and he had a great staff, including Steve Brubaker and his team. They did not just walk in and say, "Here is what it is going to be." They gave us choices.

We met with Gyo over and over again about the necessary details: how many courtrooms we needed and what they should look like; what the adjacencies needed to be; where the judges' chambers had to be in relation to the courtrooms; where the court reporters should be; where the lawyers' rooms should be placed; and where the clerks' offices should be located. We built the inside, stacked it all up, and then wrapped it.

Because we were lawyers as well as judges, we explained why we needed three rooms for the lawyers to use for

each courtroom, and HOK understood. They mocked up courtrooms and even put up balloons so that we would see the ceiling heights and imagine the sight lines. So the things we knew best, HOK picked up on and used our skills as well as their own.

While this was being designed, we visited many courthouses. Some of them looked nice, but closer examination revealed the jury box was too small, or one set of lawyers could not see the witness, or the judge's sight lines were bad. We reviewed these and supplied our

professional knowledge and expertise in trying cases to HOK, who took the information and made it work for us.

The difficult part of the project occurred when we had to cut our budget—$5 million at one whack. I think that's called value engineering. We sat down with Gyo and did it. For instance, we took a lot of wood out of the judges' offices and other such things, but we never did anything that took away from the significance of the building. We all agreed that if anything had to be made a little better, it had to be the courtrooms because that is where the people are. This building belongs to the people. It is where they come for redress of a grievance and the courtrooms are essentially their offices. If we had to cut anything, we cut it from the chambers and similar places. Consequently, we kept the project under budget.

The structure is made of precast concrete because it wears well. It is beautiful. People always ask, "What kind of stone is it?" When HOK told us it would be more of a rosy color, we raised our eyebrows. Now that our building is up, it feels rich and uplifting.

The building features a mezzanine and 28 numbered stories. The dome covers the top story where we keep all the mechanical equipment. We questioned the shape, the dome, and the base clad with strips of stainless steel. HOK pointed out to us that St. Louis is a dome city. There are domes everywhere. I never realized that. The Arch, a St. Louis landmark, is stainless steel. HOK wanted to replicate the cladding of the stainless steel.

The building is shaped the way it is for expandability. It can be built out on the sides if the need should ever arise. We planned the interior for both now and the long-range future. We put the courts in various places. The Circuit Court is at the top, below it is the U.S. Attorney's Office,

then the U.S. District Court. It was thought out very carefully. If we need to expand in the future, we could do that very easily as there is contiguous space. The District Court could push up, the Circuit Court could push down, and the U.S. Attorney could be relocated.

I am grateful for the people we had around us and for all of our judges. We had a great team—the judges' coordinating committee; the Clerks of the District, Circuit and Bankruptcy Courts; and the circuit architect and his assistant. Their cooperation, dedication, and enthusiasm were endless. They worked without fanfare, sought no praise, and made my job as committee chair a memorable experience.

Once people saw the building going up, interest developed. Groups would call for a tour. We had to wait until the construction crews quit to go through. During the process, the people had all kinds of questions about the courts and the law; and I realized that we needed an education center in this building.

In 2009, Justice Sandra Day O'Connor cut the ribbon on our Judicial Learning Center. Teachers bring their students on field trips to come learn about the law. They can sit in the judge's chair and in the jury box. We encourage their intellectual curiosity, and instill a knowledge and respect for the way our judicial system works.

The building is majestic—dome and all. I feel so good about it, and the eloquent way it expresses the role of the judicial system in our democracy. That is my reward.

The Honorable Edward L. Filippine, at the time of the project, was Chief Judge. He currently serves as Senior District Judge of the United States District Court, Eastern District of Missouri at the Thomas F. Eagleton United States Courthouse.

GYO OBATA: AN INVITING MEDICAL ENVIRONMENT

Washington University School of Medicine and Barnes-Jewish Hospital were going to build a new outpatient building. The interesting challenge was to make a medical building be more like a hotel— not stodgy and sterile, but bright and inviting.

Up until the Center for Advanced Medicine, doctors in different specialties were scattered across a three-city-block area of the Washington University Medical Center campus. Patients had difficulty finding their doctors. The intention was to bring all the outpatient services to this building so that patients could visit doctors and receive diagnostic treatment in one convenient location.

When we were selected for the project, we became part of a huge committee of people from the Washington University School of Medicine and Barnes-Jewish Hospital consisting of doctors from the various subspecialties and hospital administrators. Doctors from the medical school attended the weekly progress meetings. They were represented by Dr. James Crane.

We wanted to make this building inviting and accessible to the public. The whole medical center complex is in a fairly tight St. Louis urban area bordered by major streets: Kingshighway on the west, Forest Park Boulevard on the north, and Euclid Avenue on the east. Parking for outpatients became important. We created a 1,000-car parking garage across the street, connected by a bridge that patients could cross into the building. We also made a hotel entry-style arrival point where patients could be dropped off or have valet parking. We continued the hotel concept into a spacious public lobby with a skylight and connections to buildings.

Doctors are grouped together according to their subspecialty field of practice. An elevator in the lobby delivers patients to the appropriate floor. They cross over a bridge and come to a major corridor that faces north where they can actually look out. On the lower levels, they can look into the atrium. So again, movement is primary.

A medical center design has to be easily understandable because many patients are sick and get disoriented and do not need to be hassled or stressed. So, the movement and logistics to get to the right place have to be very clear and specific. Once patients arrive on the floor of the specialization area, the waiting rooms are filled with daylight and the treatment rooms, which do not have daylight, are directly behind them.

We worked closely with the doctors and with each team to set up the treatment areas. On the south side, or what we call "back of the house," the doctors have offices and labs. The patients come in from one side, are treated, and then exit that way. The doctors and nurses have space on the other side of the treatment area.

I tried to create a building that makes the environment easy to navigate, light, and inviting for people who may need medical care. Knowing that I might one day have to use the building myself was a real incentive to design a great building. Most of my doctors are members of the physician group practice at Washington University School of Medicine. When I have appointments, I ask them whether they like the space. Everybody seems happy with the building.

JAMES P. CRANE, MD: COLLABORATING FOR PATIENT CARE

Gyo is a true visionary who brought forward exciting ideas and thinking about the ideal patient care experience. The concepts he brought to the table resulted in a patient-centric model of care delivery.

The idea of creating a new ambulatory care facility goes some years back before Barnes and Jewish Hospitals merged. At the time, Barnes and Jewish were each contemplating working with Washington University Medical School to build an ambulatory care center, so there would have been two on campus. Fortunately, the two hospital boards and medical school leadership created a Steering Board to determine how to effectively rationalize both outpatient and inpatient clinical services on the medical center campus. After several months of study, the Steering Board recommended a Campus Integration Plan that would consolidate all ambulatory programs on the north side of the campus and relocate most resource-intensive inpatient services to the south campus.

With respect to outpatient care, we knew there was a great need because the campus was such a confusing and intimidating environment for patients. Navigating the medical center campus was particularly challenging for seniors, many of whom had complex and chronic medical problems that required the services of multiple subspecialists. Before the Center for Advanced Medicine was built, these subspecialists were practicing in 32 different geographic locations in multiple buildings across three city blocks. The Center for Advanced Medicine allowed us to consolidate all ambulatory care activities into a single, patient-focused building with a clear arrival point and convenient parking.

The Campus Integration Plan also called for consolidation of redundant inpatient clinical services. For example, Barnes and Jewish each had their own cardiothoracic surgery programs and we decided to bring those programs together. After careful analysis, it was decided to concentrate most inpatient care on the South Campus, partially because of the larger physical plant that could accommodate the consolidated services.

After the hospital boards approved the Campus Integration Plan, they realized that it was time to more closely integrate their two boards. And so, the Campus Integration Plan became the catalyst for the full merger of Barnes Hospital and Jewish Hospital.

LEFT Bright, airy waiting areas are not typically seen in medical buildings
RIGHT The hotel-like entrance welcomes visitors

LEFT The bright, positive environment contributes to a sense of wellness

Once the concept of the Campus Integration Plan was mapped out, we put out a Request for Proposal and HOK won the lead role for the project. In addition to the Center for Advanced Medicine on the north campus, the project included building a new consolidated emergency department on the South Campus along with new inpatient operating rooms, a cardiothoracic intensive care unit, and a new cardiac catheterization lab. These programs are located in a new building facing Kingshighway known as the Southwest Tower.

While HOK became the lead architect, because the project was so large—$480 million—two other architectural firms, Cannon and Christner, were engaged to work on component parts. This amalgam of architects worked wonderfully. We housed the architects from all three firms in a building adjacent to the campus. All of the work was done there. Once or twice a week, we would sit down with the architectural team to review their progress and make decisions.

I am not an architect, so I learned a lot about architecture, design, and construction as a result of this project. Our goal was not to just consolidate ambulatory care services on one site, but to effect a paradigm change from "physician-focused" to "patient-focused" care delivery. To achieve this, we organized the 47 adult subspecialties within our faculty group practice into multidisciplinary centers of excellence. For example, there is the Heart and Vascular Center on the eighth floor of the CAM where cardiologists, cardiovascular surgeons, and vascular surgeons work together in one location to care for patients with heart disease. In addition to physician offices, outpatient cardiac diagnostics are located on this same floor. So for the patient with a heart problem, everything is available in a single location. This multidisciplinary approach to care promotes coordination of care across disciplines, fosters innovation and technology development, and enhances teaching, all of which are part of our academic mission.

Gyo's designs for the CAM were not just pulled out of a box. He talked about how the building should be oriented to the east and west, how to use the sunlight, how to make the building more energy efficient, and how the entire campus should evolve as new buildings were added. He was right.

The initial thinking, before Gyo was involved, would have resulted in a very different configuration for the building.

We started with a potpourri of buildings with different orientations and different exterior skins. I think Gyo was looking far beyond the CAM, thinking how future buildings might evolve in relation to it, and how to develop a unified campus. That was insightful.

Gyo promoted the development of campus-wide architectural guidelines, which we still follow. They included suggestions for building placement and setback in relation to the streets and green spaces for campus enhancement. So, a new research building going up near here will have insulating green space and fit perfectly into Gyo's vision.

During the process, we went over budget. It is never good to go back to the boards for more money, but they were very supportive. The overrun was due, in part, to the speed with which all this evolved. Once the hospital boards decided to merge and the Campus Integration Plan was approved, they wanted to start the next day. Because of the budgetary challenges, we had to value engineer what we wanted to do and shelve some plans, which, in retrospect, may have been a blessing.

I found the Center for Advanced Medicine project to be a personally rewarding experience. I learned a tremendous amount. I always told Gyo and his team that some of my best days were days with them because in my full-time job, I am often solving political problems. This was a fun project overall, where I got to see something evolve from a concept, to paper, and to reality.

We opened the building over a 12-month period, beginning in late 2002. We built more than two floors of shell space in the building to accommodate future growth; however, our clinical practice has grown so rapidly that the shell space was fitted out within a few years to meet our expansion needs. Our patients love the Center for Advanced Medicine and the clinical faculty also appreciate how the

design has enhanced the way we deliver care. The building has been tremendous for our patients and has enabled us to provide higher quality care. Because we connected the Center for Advanced Medicine to an existing building, the eight-story atrium was a necessity and is a wonderful space that everyone enjoys. The Center for Advanced Medicine also served as a catalyst for improving patient flow and enhancing our patient registration and appointment scheduling systems.

One surprise occurred. When we programmed the building, we did not plan physical space for paper medical records as we had hoped to convert to electronic medical records by the time the facility opened. Our timing was off by several years, although over 90 percent of patient medical records are paperless today.

We also missed the mark on the capacity of the CAM parking structure. We had many parking consultants and felt that we had designed an adequate-sized garage with good traffic flow. What we did not realize was how sick and elderly our patients were, and how challenging it was for them to navigate that garage. We have actually expanded the garage since the original construction because it was not large enough physically.

We have had many visitors from peer medical schools including Emory, Columbia University, Yale, and Case Western, exploring development of their own ambulatory care facilities. They are amazed by the Center for Advanced Medicine and think it is an incredible facility. We are always happy to showcase the CAM with visitors from other academic institutions. When we were in the early phase of design with HOK, we traveled to other recently completed ambulatory care facilities including the University of Chicago and Northwestern Memorial Hospital. HOK was involved in some of the projects and made connections for us. We learned a great deal from those site visits including what worked well, as well as what not to do. Those interactions were so helpful and the people were so gracious to us. We try to do the same for others.

In summary, the Center for Advanced Medicine has been a huge success, transforming the patient care experience and enabling us to provide world-class care in the 21st century.

James P. Crane, M.D., is the Associate Vice Chancellor for Clinical Affairs and the Chief Executive Officer of the Faculty Practice Plan at the Washington University School of Medicine in St. Louis.

ALFRED A. ARRAJ U.S. COURTHOUSE

DENVER, COLORADO

GYO OBATA: ILLUMINATING JUSTICE

The courthouse expresses the justice system in a democracy. It embodies openness, representing the freedom inherent in a democracy, but mostly it exemplifies light. When you take the elevator up to the courtroom floors, the public corridor faces south and is bathed in airy and illuminating natural light.

We interviewed for the project with Anderson Mason Dale Architects, and the General Services Administration (GSA). The Justice Department chose HOK to design the courthouse. They wanted this building to be an example of green architecture, and to feel inviting, open, and accessible.

The inspiration for the design came out of the requirements, but we also wished to create a bright, welcoming building, filled with natural light. Denver is washed in sunlight almost 300 days a year. We positioned the building on a two-and-a-half-acre downtown site with major north and south orientation to capture that light. The north faces the Rocky Mountains. The south side, with all its glass, lets in the sun.

The courthouse has two parts: a two-story pavilion and a 10-story tower connected by an elevator core. The glassed-in main entrance sits on a platform designed to structurally withstand acts of man or nature. People come into the raised plaza, go through security in the central area, and walk to the elevator core.

The pavilion makes the courthouse approachable. It has a jury assembly room and a large special proceedings courtroom where people take the oath of citizenship. The tower contains the courtrooms, judges' chambers, jury deliberation rooms, and offices.

As people go up to the courtrooms, the public corridors face the south sun, which makes them very bright. High windows in the courtrooms take some light from the corridors and bring daylight in. Warm-colored American maple details the courtroom walls and furnishings.

To make this building a symbol of sustainable architecture, we used healthy materials, and managed the site use and the disposal of unusable materials. We designed the skin to keep the sun's energy out, but to still bring in daylight. On top of the building, we put in solar collectors. One word that best represents this building is "light." It is an appropriate metaphor for a building that is home to truth and justice.

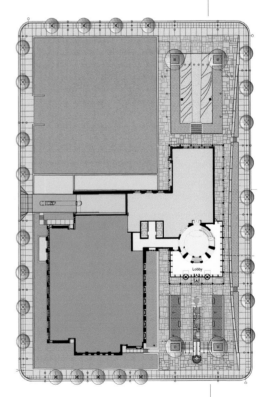

LEWIS T. BABCOCK: PROJECTS ARE ABOUT RELATIONSHIPS

There was always the consideration that the new courthouse would not compete with the Byron White Courthouse, which is classic in its architecture and clad in Colorado Yule marble, but would complement and have a dialogue with that jewel in our federal campus.

The Byron G. Rogers Courthouse was out of space, insecure in terms of prisoner transport, and mechanically out-of-date. Given our needs for court space and the federal judiciary's requirement that each court have a long-range space plan, we set out to create the Alfred A. Arraj Courthouse, which would work with the renovation of the Byron G. Rogers Courthouse.

The process of choosing an architect was collaborative. The General Services Administration (GSA) is the property owner. The federal judiciary pays rent to the GSA. One of the things that the federal judiciary has learned is that the court and its judges should be intimately involved in the planning, design, and construction of a courthouse, as they are the ones who use the building. We had a partnering session between the court and GSA.

The project was delegated to me by Judge Sherman G. Finesilver, then chief judge of the district. We had an excellent GSA project manager, and worked with GSA officials. We interviewed five architectural firms. As a result of those interviews, HOK, who was partnering with local firm Anderson Mason Dale, was selected by consensus for this project.

Once we had HOK and AMD under contract, I imparted to them the essence of the federal judiciary, and what a courthouse is, particularly a trial court. It was my sense that the courthouse should have certain attributes consonant with the function of this very important institution. It also had to relate to the neighborhood, an environment that includes the Byron White United States Courthouse, a grand edifice clad in Colorado Yule marble. There was no way that the budget would allow marble and I didn't want to compete with that beautiful building. The concept was to complement it both in massing and in style.

A federal trial court is a serious place, and its architecture should reflect that. Important work is done here; it is the people's work. People come to a court

LEFT The courthouse edifice is a new, modern symbol of justice in Denver
RIGHT The glass entrance glows at night over the plaza

when they have problems, or are charged with a crime. Here, civil disputes or criminal cases can be impartially, dispassionately resolved under the rule of law in a secure environment. The heart of a trial courthouse is the courtroom. That is where all elements of the judicial process come together in the adversarial process. It is the crucible of the process. The courthouse edifice should embody the importance of what occurs there.

Two designs were presented. The first one was a three-court-per-floor, lower vertical concept. Shortly after that design was considered and approved by GSA in Washington, the Murrah Building in Oklahoma City was bombed. All federal building designs were re-evaluated for progressive collapse, security—all those things. The site for the building drives the footprint, so we had to pull back and redesign a new concept.

We had ongoing discussions both in the Anderson Mason Dale offices and in the courtrooms, which helped to inform what we were trying to accomplish. When Gyo says projects are about relationships, he is exactly right. There are innumerable relationships critical to any project. In this instance, there were the relationships between the court and the local GSA, the Washington GSA offices, their architect Ed Feiner—a visionary who demanded good public architecture in federal courthouses without a cookie-cutter, one-size-fits-all approach—and, of course, Congress, our banker from whom we secured authorization and appropriations for site acquisition, design, and construction funding.

Once we had the design approved, we had to put it out for bid. In December 1999, we had a $10 million bid bust. The United States Marshals Service proved to be another constituent involved in the project. So I sat down with the regional GSA administrator, the head of Marshals

Service Space and Facility's Division, and our GSA project manager. We sought a way to go to contract because what is anathema to any building project is delay—and it is off. We carved out 107 separate items that were bid out as options. We went through a list of 50 or so, and were still short, so we got into a second list and got Washington and the Marshals Service to kick in more money. We deleted a floor, two courtrooms, and two chambers from the design, saved $3 million, and awarded the contract.

The process involved a partnering session. We worked for two days with the GSA, the architects, the court, the general contractors, and the prime sub-contractors. Again, I attempted to impart the importance of the building and

LEFT Pillars, a symbol of strength, are modern and steel clad
ABOVE Stairs in the rotunda are illuminated with natural light

187

LEFT The vaulted ceilings inspire reverence for the justice system

what occurs there. Establishing a very collegial working relationship with all the parties involved paid dividends. While Curtis Berg, the GSA Project Manager, had the final yea or nay on any questions, I can only think of maybe a half a dozen or so where he had to do that, because we would arrive at solutions by consensus. He made it work.

What stands out most in my mind is the camaraderie among all those people involved in the process. We had fun while we did it. We were friends when it ended and could take pride in our accomplishment. During the process, I always felt warmly toward Gyo. Although he was not at every one of the planning meetings, other HOK architects were there. I always hoped that he would be there and was always glad when he was.

Once, we had a hard time coming to a decision about the finish in our woodwork. We didn't want it too dark and we didn't want it too light. We were at AMD's office and there was discussion about something like caramel. One of the architects brought a little piece of caramel candy and set it down. We said, "Eureka, perfect!" And that is the way we finished it.

Our vision for the building was met. In the upper downtown area, back in the '70s and '80s, a lot of fine old buildings were torn down and replaced with new glass buildings. The lower downtown area retained some of its historical architectural expression. We gave architectural expression to the front of the building that relates to the new part of the downtown area. We thought we could clad it in limestone, but because of budget issues, we used brick that communicates with the lower downtown area.

From the onset, we thought that the courthouse should not be just a high-rise. We attached the pavilion, which references the public image of the courthouse in the town square. That pavilion lends a massing that communicates with the Byron White building. We had some trouble figuring out how to complement that building. Someone identified a project in Nice, France, where a new glass and metal building is juxtaposed with an ancient Roman structure. We took that as our lead and designed the pavilion, which expresses, "This is a courthouse."

A number of us had toured new courthouses around the country. I noticed that the special proceedings courtroom where investitures occur, where trials are still held, and where people gather was high on top of the buildings. I thought we should bring the room down to a lower level because that is more egalitarian. I also thought the jury assembly room ought to be in the pavilion with the special proceedings courtroom above, so that it accomplishes these things: it welcomes people who enter the building; it gets the jurors directly into the jury assembly room; it reduces the stress on vertical transportation; and it says, "This is *your* courthouse." This belongs to the people. It is where the important public business of resolution of disputes and criminal charges occurs.

The Arraj Courthouse project changed me in this way. My father had a lumberyard in a small town in Colorado. When I was growing up, I worked there and had some experience with construction. The courthouse became like a second occupation because I was involved from 1991 until it was completed. I worked with Tom Morey, an architect who worked on behalf of the court. We attended the construction meetings. The project gave me a great appreciation for all the people involved and the opportunity to see it come to completion. The public dedication was exciting, as is the way the building relates to the federal role and the complex down here. Everyone seems pleased.

What I do as a judge is so different from what we were doing in overcoming obstacles along the way. My mother told me that there were two ways to make a living: "You can do it with a shovel or you can do it with your mind." After we completed the groundbreaking ceremony, I saved a brick from the foundation and the shovel used to dig the hole. For me the word that best describes my overall feeling about the project is "gestalt."

The Honorable Lewis T. Babcock was the Chief Judge of the United States District Court for the District of Colorado. He currently serves as a United States District Court Judge.

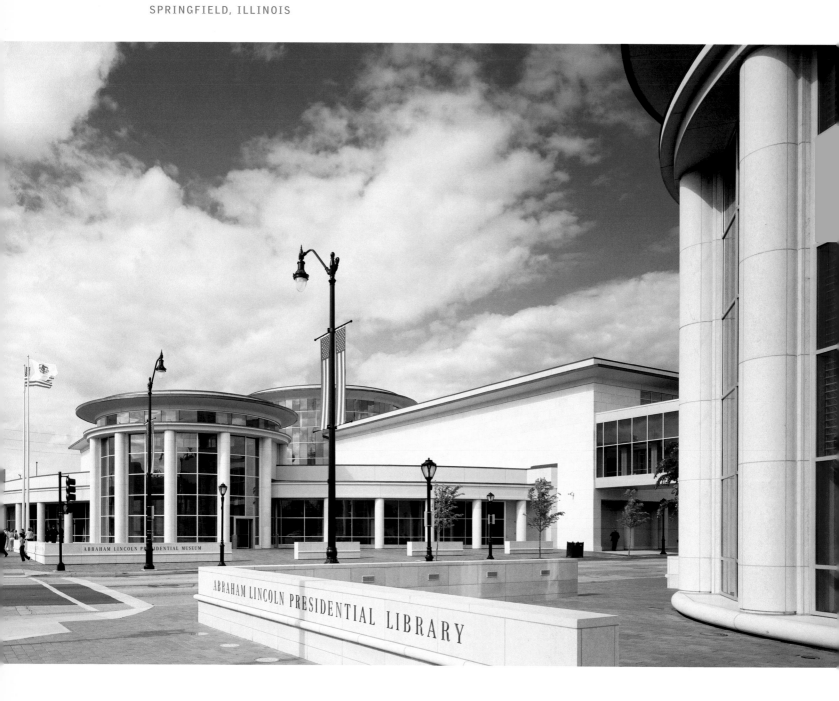

GYO OBATA: A DISPLAY OF LEADERSHIP

I consider Abraham Lincoln to have been the greatest U.S. President. To design a building for

him was a real challenge.

When the Illinois Capital Development Board sent out notices for this project to architects and engineers, we submitted our qualifications. We were among the firms invited to Springfield. The interview process was very formal and we got the job.

The State of Illinois' Historic Preservation Agency wanted a library and museum distinct from any other presidential library. Because they didn't have the document volume found in recent presidential libraries, they wanted to create an engaging experience. They went to Disney, who recommended Bob Rogers of BRC Imagination Arts, an exhibit design specialist.

This project had two parts: the library to hold historical state documents, Illinois family histories, and period documents; and the museum, which would entertain and instruct about Lincoln's life. We were not sure how much space we needed for either element. In preparation, I made hundreds of sketches and worked up images and models to gauge direction. At the time, we held meetings with 12 Lincoln scholars and asked which of Lincoln's life events should be featured.

Out of that information, the exhibit designer chose certain segments of Lincoln's life. One exhibit chronicles actions leading up to the Civil War. Lincoln's election is held as if it were happening today, with political interviews and analysts who speak about Lincoln.

This was to be a black box museum with no natural light in the exhibit area. Architects rely on light to bring form to a space. It was challenging. I created a central atrium with a skylight overhead that provides a navigational place for visitors. From there, people go to each of the exhibit areas to experience Lincoln's early life or his life in Washington, D.C.

On the exterior, I designed a contemporary building that referenced traditional Illinois public buildings, many of which had columns. I searched globally and found a stone quarried in Egypt. We sent it to Italy to be made into columns. This warm beige limestone has a luminous quality.

During this project, I rediscovered Lincoln. I learned how he wrestled with difficult decisions, came to grips with the question of emancipation, and grew into a better person. He taught me again about leadership and its complexities.

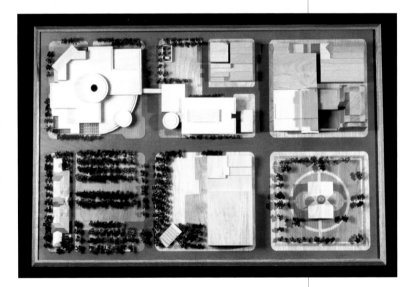

JULIE CELLINI: A STORY-DRIVEN MUSEUM EXPERIENCE

Illinois has a marvelous Lincoln collection that has grown since we opened the museum.

I am Chairman of the Board of Trustees for the Illinois Historic Preservation Agency. I also am Secretary of the Abraham Lincoln Presidential Library and Museum Foundation. In addition, I serve as a Co-chairman of the Illinois Bicentennial Commission and am a member of the Federal Abraham Lincoln Bicentennial Commission, so I am certainly knee-deep in Lincoln.

When we decided to build the new buildings, we began with a large committee of staffers from the Illinois Historic Preservation Agency who, like me, have long known the Lincoln sites. Senator Dick Durbin was part of that. We all agreed from the start that this museum needed to be different from those that display things in glass cases. It was always underpinned by the Illinois collection that gave it the authenticity and certainly the research materials, but we wanted to tell Lincoln's story in a worthy way.

The Capital Development Board, the building arm of the Illinois government, chose the architect from among 26 submittals. It was the largest number of firms that had ever bid on a Capital Development Board project. The 10 of us on the selection committee culled the group several times. Everyone read all the proposals and certainly followed the Capital Development Board's guidelines and pre-qualifications—the kinds of things that a good government project does. Eventually, I think, there were six firms that presented to us. HOK was one of them.

The reasons we chose HOK were many, not the least of which was that Gyo was a principal. Gyo delivered the presentation. He spoke movingly about his life-long dedication and fascination with Lincoln. He tied in his own remarkable story of being a college student when World War II broke out, and the internment camps in California. He attended Berkeley at the time and talked with his parents about transferring to a part of the country that would feel more welcoming to an Asian American. He came to Washington University in St. Louis.

He shared his enduring feeling for the Midwest, and how he established his firm in the Midwest because it was a more tolerant and open place for someone of his heritage and with his professional goals as an architect. He drew the parallel with Lincoln, and how Lincoln came to Illinois, establishing himself first at New Salem and then in Springfield.

RIGHT The low-scaled complex creates a lively streetscape
LEFT Light-filled rotundas, like display cases, draw in visitors

It was a magical time and I always felt privileged to be part of the project. The vision was collective, never one person's idea. The thought was, "Let's tell Lincoln's story in a way that is relevant to 21st-century audiences." It included both the experience inside the museum and the architectural expression.

The public offered a great deal of commentary about the project during town hall meetings held in Springfield. Some people felt that because the dome of the old Capitol is red and Springfield has red brick buildings dating back to Lincoln's era, the building should be all red brick. Gyo gave us a timeless building that fits in a historic downtown. It was appropriate the day it first opened and it will be appropriate 100 years from now.

Gyo did not borrow from downtown Springfield. He gave us a building that is recognizable, stately, modern, and timeless. If he keyed off anything, it was the marble coloration, which complements the old state Capitol in the center of downtown, just a block away. The public is very complimentary about the building's appearance and the experience it offers.

From the start, Gyo and HOK were comfortable that the experience inside the museum would take the lead. This combination library and museum is unlike any other. We toured the country, sometimes accompanied by Gyo. We looked at historic sites and presidential libraries and gleaned a lot of information, but never found a model for what we hoped to create.

Simply sitting on the committee that worked with BRC Imagination Arts of Burbank, California, was most exciting. Everyone on that team had the remarkable experience of seeing the Lincoln story take shape in accordance with our goal of reaching our audience emotionally in order to reach them intellectually. The museum experience is, of course, story driven. Is there a better story in all of American history? The son of a Kentucky dirt farmer advances to the U.S. Presidency and saves the nation. That was the storyline we worked on with BRC Imagination Arts.

Gyo infused that concept throughout the buildings he created. We would have loved to have had more space in order to tell the story in even greater detail, but we were in a confined space in a downtown area. Gyo worked well with the space limitation. The theatre space called for large walls without windows and the placing of a clerestory at the top, so that the rotunda is bathed in natural light. All those things add to the visitor experience and fulfill the promise of our design intention.

When I am at the museum, I think about the surprise of the Lincoln pennies. When visitors enter, there is a small rotunda and a large, grand rotunda as they go into the theatre. In both of those, Gyo designed a beautiful marble floor with various colored marble on the radius emanating to the center. The centers of both rotunda circles are inlaid with Lincoln pennies. That was not part of the initial design. It was something the people who laid the floors decided to do.

All along the way, there were surprises. We watched drawings actually come to life. We knew the spaces would be grand and filled with story, and how people would move through them because Gyo kept us informed. I give tours and am still awed. I have all the stories about what happened where and why during the design and construction. They are fun to share. But mostly, people want to know the story of Lincoln. This building is a narrative that interprets that story well.

LEFT A research place, befitting a president with a far-reaching legacy
RIGHT The library's gallery-like central axis is bright and light-filled

The structure's pillars and configurations evoke Lincoln's strength; the windows and clerestory suggest illumination. The building embodies what he was able to do for this country through the *Emancipation Proclamation*. We tell the story of how his own Cabinet did not fully agree with him. And yet he believed that the Union must go on.

Before we had our beautiful, HOK-designed library and museum, we could only offer visitors the historic Springfield pieces of the Lincoln story—a mosaic of the 30 years Lincoln spent in Illinois. Now, with the completion of the library, we are able to give them the whole picture of Lincoln's life.

I do not think the project changed anyone who worked on it. Our historians, led by Illinois State Historian Tom Schwartz, were grounded in Lincoln and sure of all aspects of the story. Perhaps it simply deepened everyone's commitment, including that of our foundation board.

The board has since purchased a huge Lincoln collection to add to the state's Lincoln collection. We now have probably the most significant Lincoln collection in private hands. Scholars are using it. Materials from it are on display. Lincoln's hat was purchased in that collection and it is there and on display because of the museum. We would not have had things like this without a museum in which to display them, and a library to collect, archive, and preserve the materials.

People have made significant donations to the museum's collection. Lincoln's briefcase—a satchel with his name on it that might have carried the *Emancipation Proclamation* back and forth from the summer house—was donated by a family who learned about the library museum. It enhanced our ability to tell the Lincoln story.

We began with a vision that whatever Gyo and HOK were going to design had to be worthy of Lincoln. We were convinced at the onset that Gyo and his firm would give us what we wanted, and they did not disappoint. The look and flow of the buildings have met that goal. All pieces relate holistically. You cannot separate the experience that people have in the library and in the museum from the buildings that house them. It is not unusual to see visitors photographing Gyo's beautiful buildings—as well as the Lincoln statues. We are the envy of many places because of Gyo, HOK, and BRC Imagination Arts. We invite everyone who reads this book to visit Springfield and see for themselves.

Julie Cellini is the Chairman of the Board of Trustees for the Illinois Historic Preservation Agency. She also is Secretary of the Abraham Lincoln Presidential Library and Museum Foundation, Co-chairman of the Illinois Lincoln Bicentennial Commission, and member of the Federal Abraham Lincoln Bicentennial Commission.

GYO OBATA: FORM, FUNCTION, AND FLOW

Washington University has one of the top medical schools in the United States, but its facilities were not well organized. The students had to go from building to building. I wanted to design a facility that would be open and filled with light, creating a pleasant environment for them. I think light is really an important part of this building.

We were interviewed, selected for the project, and asked to design a new "heart" for the medical school. It would include high-tech lecture halls, laboratories, classrooms, and study areas, and be positioned on a very tight site. Working closely with a committee of professors, facilities people, and students, we determined the kinds of spaces they found workable. The site used to be one of the utility plants for Barnes Hospital. To the north was an old, traditional structure that housed some of the medical school facilities.

The site was selected because it was close to the library, the medical library, and other buildings where students attended classes and laboratories. Because it was a very tight site, we obtained permission to close Scott Avenue in order to connect the new building with the old north building. We put a roof with skylights over the street to create a pedestrian walkway from Euclid Avenue toward the east. It tied together the medical school, the library, and the new building.

We created small-, large-, and full-scale models of classroom spaces. Some of the classrooms had to be flexible enough to expand into larger classrooms. Our interior designers gathered information on how high the counters should be, how the microscopes would be used, and other medical details. In addition, we created spaces where the doctors and students could meet and talk. Students walking on Euclid can enter the building and enjoy the dining area.

The building is six stories; the students are on four stories. In order to relate it to the existing building, we used beige brick, glass, and limestone. I created a tower on the corner of Euclid and Scott with lounge areas where students and clinical and research doctors can visit and view Forest Park.

I am an alumnus of Washington University and I know that the medical school is a great one. We had an opportunity to enrich the physical environment and make it conducive to learning and interaction among students, teachers, and doctors. Movement from the medical center, the clinical research areas, and back to the school became pivotal.

LEFT The new, covered galleria unites the library and the new medical school

WILLIAM A. PECK, MD: ARCHITECTURE'S ENERGIZING EFFECTS

The entrance area is elevated at the top of the building. It is an entrance facade. When you realize that this is a building devoted to learning and to education, the entrance enhances that importance.

When we began to contemplate in detail our educational mission for the Washington University School of Medicine, we realized that there was a great need for expanded, attractive, and functional facilities. We wanted to link formal medical education at the basic science level, clinical level, and graduate student level to the lifestyle of the students that populate the medical center. The building would be a way of bringing the faculty and the students more closely together informally, but also would sharply expand our formal education spaces.

We recognized that a transformation of medical learning is occurring through small-group education, the use of simulators, dramatic expansion of the use of information technology, communications technology, and so forth. We needed new lecture halls and gathering places all in a single building. I appointed a student-faculty committee headed by Philip Stahl, Ph.D., one of our department heads. The committee consisted of three board members, three trustees, faculty, and students.

We came up with the concept of a learning and teaching center that would provide not only new spaces for advanced approaches to education, but that would also be a hearth, a gathering place, and an opportunity for expanded, informal interactions. We were aware that several other medical schools had undertaken such a development of spaces—Harvard being the first. Other schools were also in the process of building facilities that would accomplish at least some of those goals.

LEFT The covered entrance and walkway at dusk

The committee developed a concept plan that we wanted to pursue. All of the relevant university committees approved it. The Chancellor and the Washington University Board of Trustees were very excited about it. After we developed it, the time came to find an architect. A Request for Proposal was distributed and a number of architectural firms applied.

We recognized that Washington University School of Medicine ranked first in the nation in student selectivity, which is a composite of the performance of students in college in terms of grade-point average, performance on the Medical College Admissions Test, as an aggregate, and the number of students we had to offer positions to fill our classes as a percentage of applications. I wanted to preserve and continue to enhance the quality of our students. I felt that this building would do that. Also, it is fair to say that healthcare is changing dramatically, and continues to do so, as it advances in the understanding of disease and health. We wanted to provide the most modern educational opportunities, and we needed a new building to do that.

There was a meeting of the overall planning committee and we heard reports from the site-visit teams that had talked with and interviewed the candidate architectural firms. We recognized that HOK was one of the few world leaders in architecture and also happened to be headquartered locally, although their local base was not an issue. Of course, in addition to being local, they are one of the best. Everybody knows that. They have done educational and healthcare facilities everywhere, from Saudi Arabia to the Pacific Rim, and many projects in the St. Louis region.

And so it was felt that the design potential and the site visit information offered by HOK would give us a thrilling building that would be a centerpiece of the medical center. It would be a front door, a portal of entry for all of the School of Medicine's activities. The design was truly ingenious.

Almost all of the design was done under my deanship, but it was not finalized until after I stepped down. In 2003, construction began. The building is now up and running. It bears the name The Farrell Learning and Teaching Center, after David and Betty Farrell, and has more than fulfilled our expectations. It is a very attractive front door to a medical school, and has wonderful spaces for education and for informal communication that are heavily used. It is a stunning building that helps us attract students and faculty, and it is fun to be in.

The location of the building allowed us to close off a segment of Scott Avenue, because part of the structure was really an existing wall of a medical school building. Of course, money is saved by not having to build one wall. The gathering space is the largest interior space, a covered-over segment of an enclosed section of Scott Avenue. We had used that approach before when we built the Bernard Becker Medical Library.

When people walk into the building, they get a great feeling. It is nice to be in. It is a pleasant space, capacious but not enormous. I have taught there and it is a wonderful place to teach. The students love it. They have parties and receptions there. It has become the centerpiece for the medical school, and is the "go to" place for the students.

The most exciting element of the project was that it made a statement on behalf of the medical school and university about the importance of our educational mission. Undergraduate medical education, that is the education of medical students, is the only unique function of the medical school. We do research, we provide patient care, we provide community service, and we do those things at a very high level with great excellence. We are one of the best in all of those areas.

Those activities are pursued by entities in addition to medical schools. Free-standing teaching hospitals can do all of those things. Research institutes can do a lot of those things. But a medical school is the place where students learn to become physicians, and this facility was the first major statement of the importance of that activity for our school.

I was dean for 14 years. With that kind of experience, almost nothing surprises me anymore. During those years, we added 600,000-700,000 square feet to the campus.

It was a lot of space. But I guess what did surprise me was the fact that the building exceeded my expectations.

Although I was not really involved in the day-to-day process of working with Gyo and HOK, I got reports and they were positive. I am biased because I feel the team is one of the most imaginative in modern architecture. I chaired the Search Committee for the Deanship of the School of Architecture that concluded its activities about a year ago, so I became more appreciative during that process of how major architecture entities operate and the importance of the design process.

New buildings energize academic communities. This building allowed us to broaden and expand our mission. To me, that was the most exciting thing.

The building is centrally located. A bridge connects it to the rest of the medical center. From the building, we can get to the hospitals, to the rest of the medical school, to the library, and so forth. Essentially, we can walk from one end of the campus to the other end without getting wet. The central location constantly reminds us of our ultimate purpose, which is to improve healthcare through patient services, education, and research. It brings all our missions together. To a certain extent that had been accomplished by a prior building, the Eric P. Newman Education Center, devoted basically to continuing education. But what this new building did was position medical education as the centerpiece. We learned that if you want to have a great building, you hire a great architect. It is as simple as that.

William A. Peck, M.D., at the time of the project design, was the Dean of the Washington University School of Medicine in St. Louis. He is currently the Director for the Center of Health Policy and the Alan A. and Edith L. Wolff Distinguished Professor of Medicine.

GYO OBATA: A PLAN TO FOSTER INNOVATION

People can go from the famous Wrigley Building on Michigan Avenue, get on a boat,

and come up to the Global Innovation Center on the Chicago River.

At age 34, Bill Wrigley became head of Wrigley after his father's sudden death. Interested in doing more than making gum, he also wanted to consolidate several offices into a single collaborative workspace.

The site was on Goose Island, surrounded by the Chicago River. It sat beyond the downtown area, near industrial buildings and warehouses, where the river meanders to the northwest and barges turn around. Although it was beautiful, it was not used well.

For our first project meeting, I brought pictures of Venice with all the wonderful buildings along the canal. I said, "Chicago should do something like this. It would rejuvenate the Chicago River." Given Chicago's very cold winters and hot summers, I thought of creating a central winter garden with plants and flowers bordering the labs and offices. Bill loved the idea.

The Wrigley Company is located on all the continents. Bill wanted one garden area for each of the regions in the world, with plants native to those places. Joe Karr, a Chicago landscape architect, worked with us.

Over the garden, we put a thin skylight so people could see the Chicago skyline. Inside, we placed a water feature at the entry and a series of tables. In the corner, I created a lounge, a meeting area, and a library.

I wanted the exterior surface to be light, so we used a beautiful beige stone from Minnesota called Kasota. We painted the window trim red to make the building sparkle. The building also features a tower that resembles a lighthouse.

We met 24 times to review plans and to find the best solutions. Bill showed tremendous interest and involvement in all aspects of this project, from the materials, to the furnishings, colors, fabrics, and floors. He cared about the Wrigley culture and environment. This inspired me as an architect. I am pleased that Bill is happy about the building and hope it will help accomplish his vision of innovation.

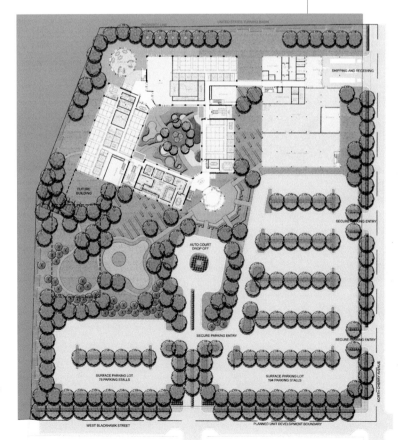

LEFT The Global Innovation Center faces and embraces the Chicago River

WILLIAM WRIGLEY, JR.: A PLACE WHERE PEOPLE CHANGE THE WORLD

Great things can be created with the right kinds of relationships. It still comes back to relationships and respect. With that and a little bit of time, it is just unbelievable what you can do.

The project started in 2000, as I began running the company. We knew we had to do some things differently. There would have to be changes for there to be future success. We were in a new, competitive environment with new challenges.

One compelling issue we faced was the need to be more innovative. We made the spirit of innovation a core principle and one of our top four goals. We focused on it while promoting a sense of urgency, communication, and measured risk.

One of the outcomes of this focus was the creation of a space where we could develop more products and processes. Our research and development hub was in Chicago, sandwiched in an old factory between manufacturing floors. The space was inadequate; the equipment was inadequate. We needed a different space.

We found a site on Goose Island. At the onset, I was not too involved in the process. A group of engineers and manufacturing folks came to me with a building design for my approval. It was a design HOK had done and I rejected it. It did not accomplish the vision and objectives that Dr. Surinder Kumar, our Chief Innovation Officer, and I had set forth.

I am not sure we had communicated our vision. I wasn't too involved at the beginning, but I got involved and started interviewing architects. Frankly, it was not a great process. My experience with architects with whom I've dealt is that most of them have egos bigger than the buildings they build, and they design for themselves, not their clients. At a lot of the meetings, I sat and listened to people who were not doing a lot of listening. I remember one meeting, walking in and in the first five minutes one guy said, "I only work in glass and steel." I said, "Okay, thank you very much." It was disappointing. Somewhere along the line, Surinder said, "HOK wants to come back to the project. Gyo Obata wasn't involved in the early process. He would like to come talk to us." I said okay.

It was a totally different meeting. Gyo is soft-spoken, understated, and has humility, all of which are characteristics that, if you have been around for any length of time, you respect and recognize immediately. Such characteristics suggest underlying strength and capability, which breed confidence. If people are not humble and soft spoken, typically they are hiding something and making up for an inadequacy. It was clear that Gyo was a good guy. That was revelation number one, which was new to me in the evaluation process.

Second, what happened was Gyo listened and wanted to know more about what we wanted to accomplish. Interestingly, Surinder and I are visionary, and very culturally oriented. We rallied our people around the soul of the company. We are very values- and principle-driven.

This company is guided that way. There is a lot of emotion, heritage, and history. So, we did not want to discuss building size, dimensions, or equipment with an architect. We wanted to talk about what the building should feel like.

Gyo picked up on that instantly. He understood we were talking about reinforcing and moving the Wrigley Company culture forward with this building. It was a pivotal time for our company. We were not trying to build a landmark building. We were concerned about how people would feel working in this building, this hub that we were creating in Chicago. Our first conversations had little to do with the building itself. Out of that process, we decided to move forward and work with Gyo.

HOK is lucky to have Gyo and to have received another chance. I am lucky too. I learned that sometimes it pays to give people a second chance. We decided to set up a small lead design team consisting of Surinder, Carol McLysaght, a key staff person, Gyo, and me. We met frequently for three-hour chunks outside of the office. It is hard for executives to assume a creative mindset and be inspired to make something happen in an office setting. We needed a different venue.

We met frequently in the board room of a quaint hotel in Lake Forest near my home. We talked about the building and generated ideas. Gyo would listen and we would listen to Gyo. We had that respect, and we were able to constructively critique each other's work to achieve the best possible outcome. So often in the world of architecture, when people put their ideas on the table, they are not receptive to constructive change. While none of us has the best idea, we also don't want to give up on an idea. Sometimes we have to explain something. I would challenge Gyo on something and he would explain his reasoning. Gyo was receptive to my questions, criticisms, and new ideas. That receptivity breaks down a lot of barriers.

From the onset, our working relationship was like a good marriage, where it doesn't matter what is thrown at you. We could come to those meetings and have fun working through issues. We did have issues at various times about how much it was going to cost. We are a public company and could not just build the Taj Mahal, so we did our share of value engineering.

Through our very open and dynamic process, we ended up with a design that reflects the vision, culture, values, principles, collaborative spirit, and soul of our company. It speaks to diversity, even with our plantings. People come from different parts of the world and say, "It is not just Wrigley Chicago. Wrigley Asia is here in some way."

We represent the globe here and wanted people to be inspired by the space. We bring customers and suppliers here. People can feel the warmth, light, and energy through the skylight. They can see the transparency in the windows, enjoy the environment, and marvel at the way everyone can see each other. The tower is a lighthouse and a beacon of innovation for the company. People look at that and point to this building.

This building is more than an innovation center. We have built something of great significance to the culture, legacy, and soul of this company. I was recently asked if architecture changes the world. I said, "No, people do." Architecture helps create the environments in which people change the world. An inspiring environment draws the right people who enhance the culture and make great things happen. This is what is happening here in this building.

ABOVE The Winter Garden provides casual, sunny areas to meet

Two exciting moments occurred at the same time on this project. After we had sketched the building with its winter garden, lighthouse, and almost kite-like formation, we had our "aha!" moment and said, "This is it!" Everyone had contributed something meaningful to our successful and grand collaboration.

The second exciting moment occurred on that same day when I brought my young daughter to the meeting. She sat at the table with us and colored and drew while we conversed. Gyo, who is such a gentleman, was great. He treated her like anyone else in the room. If she asked a question, he would stop and patiently explain. When we showed her the final design, we had the endorsement of the next generation.

Sometimes the toughest part is to get to the design; that is where the project really begins. Gyo immersed himself in the project details and kept us involved. We are fairly detail-oriented as an organization, so we selected colors and finishes. Everyone saw the project through to completion without handing it off to someone else to execute, which informed the essence of the effort and maintained the continuity, vision, and feel. The result was a complete and successful project.

I reflect back fondly on the collaboration we enjoyed as a team, bringing this building to life, and admire how we created this, and how things fell into place. I carry the lessons of purposeful team dynamics forward into other projects.

I am the luckiest guy in the world. I get to run this great company and travel the world inspiring people. I work with terrific people in different cultures who do great things that positively impact people's lives. I am proud of the company

and its people. I am proud that this building serves as a beacon of innovation, as symbolized by the lighthouse tower and expresses the soul, values, and principles of our company in 182 countries around the world. It is impressive to walk in and meet a customer, a team from Asia, or a team from Europe, and hold a meeting in the Winter Garden. This project is about those relationships and conversations, and the great things that grow out of them. We created an environment for people to bring ideas into reality. It is inspiring.

William Wrigley, Jr., at the time of the project, was Chief Executive Officer and Chairman of the Board. The company was purchased by Mars Incorporated in 2008.

CENTENE PLAZA

ST. LOUIS, MISSOURI

GYO OBATA: PROMINENT DESIGN, PRIME LOCATION

The site is the most prominent corner in Clayton, Missouri, and Michael Neidorff wanted
us to create an urban place for people to work and enjoy.

I heard that Centene Corporation was going to get involved on this important site at the corner of Forsyth Boulevard and Hanley Road in Clayton, Missouri. Michael Neidorff, the Chairman and Chief Executive Officer, wanted to create both an office building and a gathering place with shops, restaurants, and outdoor attractions. We interviewed and were selected.

This was a challenging site for two office buildings and a garage; it was critical that they fit into the skyline appropriately. After many schemes, we decided that there will be a restaurant with indoor and outdoor dining between the office and the garage. A special canopy, an art object by Liam Gillick, will connect the garage to the main office lobby. Next to that will be trees. A water wall similar to the one at Paley Park in New York City, a fire pit for evening gatherings, and a small bar will energize the space.

The office building is 17 stories of glass from floor to ceiling. Centene will occupy eight or nine floors and Armstrong Teasdale will have five. In preparing for the project, we flew to New York and looked at buildings with the latest glass technology. Unlike most, this building is not as reflective, so it will look glassy. Silkscreen-patterned glass will control sunrays on the west, south, and east sides. Darker glass in some areas will ensure privacy.

My design philosophy is to design a good building that relates to its community. This building's location, courtyard, arrival area, and impact on Clayton will distinguish it from

any in St. Louis. It will be the region's most contemporary, high-tech structure.

I want to design buildings that are almost minimalist. I have tried to maintain that focus without interruption. To create a community of offices and retail in one of the most important sites in the metropolitan area with Michael Neidorff has been rewarding. And everyone who works here will enjoy the building's airy brightness and its relationship with the outdoors.

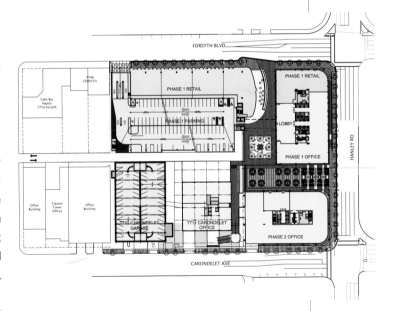

MICHAEL NEIDORFF: ENVISIONING A TRANSFORMATION

You have to be sensitive to the environment and to everybody around you.

That is what I think about.

As the Chairman, President, and Chief Executive Officer of the Centene Corporation, I realized that we needed space. We are growing rapidly. We own this building and then we bought the former Library Limited. We used it, modified it, cleaned it up, and probably had 250 people working in it. Then we realized that we needed even more space.

We are blessed to be growing responsibly and quickly. We decided, "Why not build a building?" We like to control where we live; there are fewer problems in the long term. So, we tore the project apart until we got it right. Now it is financed and under construction.

At the onset, we went through a full Request for Proposal process; it had to be competitive. We had a good competition. Although I know Gyo and have confidence in him, we had to do everything competitively.

There was a small group that looked at the proposals, but I reserved the right to have an Abe Lincoln Cabinet meeting. Do you know what that is? One day in a meeting, Lincoln said, "Everybody say, 'aye.'" And they all said, "aye." And he said, "The nays have it." We are much more balanced than that here, but we joke about it. The decision was a hands-down consensus. Everybody in the group was confident that Gyo was the right one. I recognized that. So when his quote was competitive, there was no other decision. I was glad that he was successful.

We wanted to have a signature building for the region, a landmark building. They refer to Forsyth and Hanley as "Main and Main." So, whatever we do here is important to the area. We also wanted retail and a destination spot, beyond just the office building.

The design process with Gyo and HOK was a very iterative process. We saw a series of schemes. They showed us one building and I said, "We do not want one big building. We want two towers. We don't want one building that is so large that nothing else around us would probably be built that size." We wanted it to fit in and to be a very distinct building. In terms of the size, we wanted the initial tower to be about the height of the buildings around us: the Interco Tower and the Pierre Laclede Center. The second tower will be a little higher, but it will still have symmetry.

During the design process, there were no surprises once we got the land acquisition out of the way. Gyo is such a consummate professional. And it happened that we lived on the same street. After the decision was made, I would see him out walking every morning when I would be on my way to work. He would stop and have a chat about how something was going. That was fun. Then I moved, so now we have to do that by phone and by the plan basis. And any time he comes, he has the models. He explains his vision, and he is inclusive with people he has talked to and who ask about it.

Creative, thoughtful, beyond competent, fun, and in possession of a rich heritage are how I would describe Gyo. He has a very deep understanding and comprehension of the world around him. This probably leads to the quality work we are seeing and that he has done all of his life. And the truth is, he is a delight to work with. From the

RIGHT Retail, dining, and plazas create a vibrant street life

very beginning, other than when it came to the selection of artwork, I wanted it to be his building. When it is all said and done, I told the contractors, developers, and everybody else, that if there is a decision to be made and Gyo feels one way and they feel another way, Gyo wins. He has to be afforded that respect. There were things that I wanted, such as designing for security in the building, and all of us were able to work that out. And it is still his building. I have never heard anyone say anything negative about a Gyo Obata building.

For me, it is exciting to see the project rising up out of the ground after all of our effort. I like watching the crane in action, and seeing it get raised as the building gets taller during construction. We have only 14 floors left to build, but it won't be until they start to put the glass curtain on the building that it will really feel like our vision is becoming real. Right now, it is just beginning to go up—tangible but not yet complete.

What stands out about this project is that it has been a smooth process. As we all collaborate and build this building, we have experienced no consternation or problem with the architect or builder. Everybody likes each other. Everybody knows each other. It is all St. Louis and I think that is important. And, we all have one objective: to build a world-class building that will be our headquarters, as well as offer space for other businesses here in town. At every level, my vision has been clearly met.

The image that this project suggests to me is that of a neighborhood. It will have restaurants, an ice cream parlor, little waterfalls, and a fire pit. When we first moved into town, I liked taking the kids for ice cream on Sunday nights, so I wanted an ice cream parlor. There is going to be a fountain too. I want to keep young kids around, so we designed it to be safe. And on a cool evening, the fire pit will be a fun place to sit by and relax or wait for a table before going into a restaurant. There will be some retail that employees will find convenient. I want a few things for people to enjoy that create warmth and ambiance and lend a stabilizing influence to the area.

When we were first married, my wife and I lived in Toronto near two towers connected by a mall with fine stores, movie theatres, restaurants, dry cleaners, and a full supermarket. We are not going to do that here. But what I liked about that was at night, when cities tend to empty, there was activity around, with restaurants and things that people wanted to come to see and do, instead of a dark, desolate corner. This site at night can be alive.

In this kind of project, it is very important to build things that continue to live and don't become dated. It is about having a visionary like Gyo involved who can capture what you are trying to achieve and run with it in a responsible, sensitive way and come up with a product that is going to be incredible for the community. At the end of the day, it is going to transform this corner and this area. It is going to change the epicenter.

Michael Neidorff is the Chairman, President, and Chief Executive Officer of the Centene Corporation.

GYO OBATA: A REGAL EDIFICE IN GLASS

It was John Barrett's vision to place the tower on 3rd Street. It will be a crowning achievement.

In Cincinnati, 4th Street is the major street for office buildings. One block south is 3rd Street, with the Ohio River just beyond. My client, John Barrett, is the Chief Executive Officer of Western & Southern Financial Group and one of the city's top leaders. Always a champion for the city, John believes that Cincinnati should build toward the river.

When we first began the Queen City Square project 20 years ago, our initial studies placed the major building on 4th Street. But John kept saying, "We should put the main tower on 3rd Street with a beautiful entrance on 4th Street." We built a 20-story building on 3rd Street with a lower-floor parking garage and upper-floor offices. For the second phase, we planned the taller, 41-story tower on 3rd Street. John found a major corporate tenant for that million-square-foot space. The high-rise will stand 660 feet above street level, and is now under construction.

The building is floor-to-ceiling glass. It is a mixed-use space in the sense that the ground level has restaurants and retail, but it is essentially an office building. As it goes up the tower to the crown, it sets back slightly.

Cincinnati has always been known as the Queen City. I wanted to place a crown on this building and began researching queens' tiaras. The crown presented a major structural problem. We worked to make it graceful, wind-friendly, and illuminated.

I am excited to have a client so committed to the city. John has been tremendous to work with over the years. He is a leader with vision. It is his life force that made the Queen City Square project happen.

When people drive to Cincinnati from the airport in Kentucky, they see the city skyline as they cross the river. The building on 3rd Street will be very visible, especially at night, with the lighted crown. It will be the city's tallest, most contemporary office building.

LEFT Artist rendering shows Queen City Square and the Cincinnati skyline
ABOVE The completion of Phase I hints at its grand nature

223

JOHN BARRETT: A DREAM OF GROWTH; A POINT OF PRIDE

This project will be the jewel in the crown of the Queen City. It will be the focal point. If we ever get our Sunday or Monday Night Football game again, that is what you will see.

About 20 years ago, Gyo and I started dreaming about creating a superb building in Cincinnati. At that time, I was Chief Financial Officer and soon-to-be President of Western and Southern. I am now the Chairman, President, and Chief Executive Officer, and I love it. We always wanted to do something unique and special for our city. We wanted to make a good inflationary investment. Rental real estate is about as good a guard against inflation as you can get.

The cities of America are in decline. The suburban sprawl has really changed the face of America. People do not realize what they lose when they lose their roots. Many, many people never visit where they were born, where their parents lived, or where they grew up, even though they may live just 20 minutes away.

I am a firm believer that the American city needs to be great to keep the great institutions alive. We cannot move art museums and music halls about haphazardly. We should not move them to places that serve one population and exclude everyone else. We have to regard our cities as important. We felt that this $400 million project would demonstrate our commitment to the American city. We convinced another Fortune 500 company, Great American Insurance, to stay in and relocate its headquarters into our building, despite the economic advantages they would have by moving into another county. We felt it was a win-win deal, but it took guts because people said, "You can't do that anymore."

At the onset of the project, our former development partner and I selected the architect. We traveled the country looking at buildings designed by the world's foremost architects, based in cities like New York, Boston, Chicago, Atlanta, Philadelphia, Houston, Dallas, and St. Louis. We chose Gyo because he is an incredible architect who listens to his clients in order to build what they want and make them happy. Here is a letter written to me by Gyo on January 3, 2007, that illustrates his listening skills and collaborative spirit:

Dear John:

I have been meaning to write you ever since the announcement that The Great American Insurance Company and its resources are making the Queen City office building a reality.

It has been almost 20 years since you and I started on this project. During this time, I have always welcomed

LEFT Model shows pedestrian-level entrance and parking

your critical suggestions and found your thoughts and recommendations to be insightful and right to the heart of the matter. This has been invaluable to me, John, as we move forward in refining the project.

Queen City Square will make a strong statement about Cincinnati as having the most prominent, visible skyline and will highlight your dedication to keeping downtown Cincinnati alive and well.

I thank you for your friendship and confidence,
Gyo

We wanted a world-class building, and we wanted it to be timeless. We did not want to look at it and say, "That building was built in 2010." We also wanted it to be as sustainable as practical, and as useful and maintenance-free as possible.

Gyo is not a CAD kind of guy; he still uses a fountain pen to draw. We would sit down and he would pull out a piece of paper and we could change the design of a building in two or three minutes, which we did. Gyo and I worked out the design together. We traveled to a number of cities to visit with building managers. Those were fun trips. When a building manager would show something, Gyo would demonstrate his broad expertise and deliver cautionary asides like, "You don't want to use that stone;" or "You don't want to use that steel because it doesn't hold up." Together, we picked every material. We kept it clean and simple with as few moving parts as possible, but we wanted an angular effect. It had to be classic. Cincinnati is known as the Queen City. I told Gyo 20 years ago that we needed a crown for Queen City on our roof. He heard that and a different idea occurred to him. He came back with Princess Diana's tiara and I said, "What the heck! Why not?"

During the design process, there were no surprises because we were completely involved. I loved Gyo's personal attachment to the project. He stayed with it the whole way. He is probably the "Dean of American Architecture" right now.

Over time, I discovered Gyo has a flair about him, but he is not egotistical. I do not suffer egotists well. His architectural genius is apparent, but his approach is humble. He is not fancy; he is basic and rolls easily with simple tools like a fountain pen and tissue paper.

I recommend Gyo and his team to any developer. They were so easy to work with. They hold their clients' interests and desires paramount, over and above any design features that they might think are unique and interesting. Of all the country's architectural firms, HOK has been the easiest to work with. That is a tremendous selling point.

ABOVE The steel, stone, and glass tower will be green and low maintenance

RIGHT Night-time simulation showing the illuminated "crown"

We collaborated in our work and as a result we have a lot more freedom of design and execution than most who design buildings. The building was not contingent upon government subsidies. Less than one percent of this project was subsidized. That is awesome.

The approval process gave us the most difficulty. It was beyond our control and it was slow, but the toughest part is waiting for the project to finish. It is a column-free skyscraper, and it is going up at the rate of about a floor a week. Every day, I visit the site before work just to look at it. It is one block over from us and I can tell it is going to be stunning. I hope that when we open it on January 1, 2011, it creates a sensation. No one is building such a building now. And this one will be fully leased without Western & Southern taking very much space at all.

While this project has not changed me or our people at all, the perception of our company in the eyes of the community has been greatly enhanced. That is one of the things you do not readily recognize until you get into it. In a time when nobody seems to be doing much, people view us as a can-do company.

And I love what the project has done for our city's image and economy. We are talking about thousands of well-paid, new jobs. This is the linchpin for the Southeastern quarter of Cincinnati, which is shared with Procter & Gamble. It is the most awesome part of the city. People will soon realize that Cincinnati is one of the nicest cities in the world.

This process had several high points. In the dead of winter, we poured the concrete overnight for the base of the new building. It was a community event on a cold Saturday night and into Sunday evening. Thousands of people came to watch. Our office people served coffee. Bars served eggs, orange juice, and coffee instead of alcohol and beer. People just stood there freezing, watching the concrete pour. It went on for hours. Approximately 700 truckloads of concrete participated in a continuous pour. As three or four trucks would leave, another three or four would arrive.

Workers are now constructing this building. The elevator core is concrete and it is about two or three stories ahead of the steel. Watching the steel and the concrete go up a floor a week really just blows my mind. To hear people on the job saying, "I will be able to tell my grandchildren that I built this building," is also thrilling.

After we finish this building, assuming our business stays strong, we hope to build a new headquarters for Western & Southern. This will happen down the road. We also have plans for several other non-office-use businesses such as hotels, restaurants, and condominiums. It all becomes possible because this is the economic engine. We justified it, we built it, and now we've got it.

This whole process has caused us to reflect on our identity and purpose. The building is a bold and tangible statement that will be around for a hundred or more years. For our city, it is a point of pride. And for all of us involved, it is part of a growth story. It is reminiscent of the America of the last century where people dreamed about growth. These days, we seem to focus too much on ourselves.

This building is not about Western & Southern. It is about Cincinnati and its future. It is the manifestation of a dream that my two predecessors shared with me, that I was able to complete. We will soon have the most beautiful building in the country right here and it will retain that title for some time. We spared no detail. It is just spectacular.

John F. Barrett is the Chairman of the Board, President, and Chief Executive Officer of Western & Southern Financial Group.

226

He drew up all the plans by hand and it was cool to see him do that.

Recently, I graduated from Middlebury College, with architecture as my major. I received a broad liberal arts education, and I took all sorts of classes. I loved it and I enjoyed being a student.

I was able to watch our house being built. We would come by often, so I got to observe the process closely. Originally, we bought a house on Moydaigon and we moved all of our stuff into it. My dad decided—I guess we all decided—that it would be interesting to build our own house. So, we moved back to High Hampton, looked for property, and found this one.

I had faith in my dad. I remember that he showed me the design at the old house. During the summer, he worked a lot on it at our home in Michigan. He had a studio in the basement and I would go down there and he would explain to me what he was doing. He drew up all the plans by hand. I never really gave him much constructive feedback, because he knew what he was doing and I did not want to get in the way. For the planning, I think my mom and dad were in the front seat and I was in the back. They had some issues about what they both wanted along the way, but, in general, it went along pretty well.

The only say I had was that I wanted a floor-to-ceiling window in my room and my own drum room, separate from the house. That is what the meditation room was to be. Actually, I have never put my drums there.

I have grown up seeing my dad design and remember going downtown to the office with him when I was a kid. So, I definitely have always been aware of his role. Our earlier house was one he designed, as well as the one in Michigan, so I had already experienced living in his houses.

TOP A re-imagined barn hosts parties and family celebrations
BOTTOM Open and warm, the kitchen is a favorite gathering spot

To me, this was like another job for him. I was concentrating on school and my parents were concentrating on the house. The whole time, I knew we would eventually be in a really cool place.

For me, the most thrilling part was just going over to the house during construction and watching that process of design and drawings become something physical that could be touched. At that time, I had a bunch of friends from high school come over and we had a party in the basement. I sort of got in trouble for that. Everyone, though, was excited about the house.

Eventually, when it was built, we had a lot of parties at the barn. For a while it was every other weekend. It seemed like the whole high school would come over and my band would play. The barn had been on the property, but had burned and had a terrible, undulating asphalt floor that had to be ripped out. They basically built up a side of the barn, but kept some of the wood siding and materials.

What I really appreciate is the stucco on the outside of the house. It blends into the natural setting around it. The grass grows long in the front and back and creates a prairie-like setting. I like this house so much because it stands out from others, not only in our subdivision, but in St. Louis in general. It really doesn't look like anything you will see around here. It is very nice and set back from the road. We are in our own little, non-green grass oasis.

All of my friends love it, too. When people come to the front door, they say, "Great house!" Since we have moved in, it has become very cozy and there are little pockets of comfort around the house. When I was away at college it was nice to come home occasionally and see how the house had has evolved.

PREVIOUS A Chiura Obata painting presides in the living/dining room

My favorite spot is in my room, where there is an edge of a doorway that meets the ceiling and an adjacent wall. It brings together three different colors—yellow, green, and red—in the doorway. I chose one of the colors and my mom chose the others. The one little spot where they meet is my favorite. Each time I wake up, I see that spot.

I think that the best part of our house is that it takes into account the natural setting. In no way does it try to conform to those around it. People often do not think about what architecture and a natural setting can give to their homes. Instead of incorporating good design and landscape, they do what their neighbors do.

At the time we moved in, I was applying to colleges. I was then accepted and went off to school. For me, the old house represented my childhood and this one marks the beginning of adulthood. It is interesting to experience a house, not as a child, but as someone who is maturing. That has been very different. I guess I am more aware now, mainly because of my architectural background. It has been nice to view the house with an architectural eye.

All my life I have thought about architecture. It runs in my family. I do not think living in a home designed by my dad affected my decision to pursue architecture as a career. It has, however, definitely made me aware of home design.

Each time I return home and walk into the front door, I walk on the stones that my mom put down. All the stones are from Michigan and one line is composed of Petoskey stones. It is a very good feeling.

Max Obata is a recent graduate of Middlebury College, lives in San Francisco, and works as an architectural intern.

TOP The meditation room overlooks the peaceful gardens
BOTTOM A hand-laid stone floor welcomes family, guests, and visitors

AFTERWORD: CLARK S. DAVIS

Almost 60 years ago, Gyo Obata, George Hellmuth, and George Kassabaum founded their new design firm on a set of strong personal principles. George Hellmuth believed in diversification among clients, locations, services, and project types. George Kassabaum advocated the highest professional integrity in serving the firm's clients and communities.

As design partner of HOK, Gyo brought a remarkable, client-centered approach to the practice of modern architecture. He has demonstrated what we can achieve when a client's aspirations become our own. He is a master at questioning, listening, and understanding. Each of Gyo's design projects tells a story of a client relationship and the manifestation of that client's hopes, needs, and dreams. Gyo has proven time and time again that there truly are no great buildings without great clients.

The principles of HOK's founders have endured, helping the firm become one of the most admired in the design profession. Gyo and his partners have created a legacy of practice, as well as a portfolio of important clients and projects. Thousands of young architects and designers—many still practicing with the firm—have learned from Gyo's advice and example. His conversations with clients have become the models for many others, and his gentle, engaging approach will guide the firm for years to come.

Clark S. Davis, FAIA
Vice Chairman
HOK

AWARDS AND RECOGNITION

AWARDS

1969
Fellow of American Institute of Architects
(FAIA)

1990
Washington University
Honor Doctorate of Fine Arts

1991
Advisory Council for the Presidio in
San Francisco

1991
University of Missouri–St. Louis
Honorary Doctorate in Fine Arts

1992
Walk of Fame Award
St. Louis, Missouri

1992
The First Howard A. Friedman
Visiting Professor of Architecture
University of California–Berkeley

1993
The Lifetime Achievement Award
from Asian American Architects
& Engineers of Northern California

1989
Southern Illinois University–Edwardsville
Honorary Doctorate

1989
Levee Stone Award
Downtown St. Louis

2002
AIA St. Louis
Gold Award Honor

2008
Lifetime Achievement Award from
the St. Louis Arts and Education Council

2008
Washington University in St. Louis
Dean's Medal for the Sam Fox Awards
for Distinction

PRESENT BOARDS

Gateway Foundation

Opera Theatre

Gyo Obata has received many other design awards in addition to those listed here. He has lectured on topics regarding architecture and urban design and has served on design competition juries throughout the country. Profiles of Gyo Obata and his work have appeared in several American and foreign professional journals and he has contributed many articles that have been prominently featured in numerous magazines as well as several books.

Project Name Location	Comp. Date	Structural	Mechanical/ Electrical	HOK Team
The Saint Louis Abbey St. Louis, Missouri	1962	Weidlinger Associates	Harold P. Brehm	Gyo Obata, Jim Ham, Ty Beldner
Southern Illinois University Edwardsville Edwardsville, Illinois	1967	The Engineers Collaborative	Robert E. Hattis Inc	Gyo Obata, Bob Hagee
Neiman Marcus Houston, Texas	1969	Ellisor & Tanner, Inc	Guerro & McGuire and Leo L. Landauer & Associates	Gyo Obata, King Graf
University of Michigan Northwoods IV Housing Ann Arbor, Michigan	1969	The Engineers Collaborative	HOK	Gyo Obata, Robert Edmonds, Chester Roemer, James Agne
The Galleria Houston, Texas	1970	Ellisor & Tanner, Inc.	J.E. Guerrero, Phase I; Chenault & Brady, Phase II	Gyo Obata, Jim Fetterman, David Suttle
Anthony's Restaurant and Bar St. Louis, Missouri	1972	Becker, Becker and Pennell	William Tao & Associates	Gyo Obata, Charles P. Reay
Palo Alto Research Center Palo Alto, California	1975	Jack Gillum and Associates	Dalton, Dalton	Gyo Obata, Larry Self, Sandra Ackers, Robert Stauder
National Air and Space Museum Washington, D.C.	1976	LeMessurier Associates/SCI	HOK	Gyo Obata, Jerry Sincoff, Robert Barr, Chih-Chen Jen, Charles P. Reay
George R. Moscone Convention Center San Francisco, California	1981	T.Y. Lin International	Hayakawa Associates (mechanical); The Engineering Enterprise (electrical)	Gyo Obata, Bill Valentine, Patrick MacLeamy, Mark Otsea, Terrill Richert, Bradley James Hill, Jeanne MacLeamy, David Rizzoli
Levi's Plaza San Francisco, California	1982	Cygna Consulting Engineers	Vann Engineering (mechanical); The Engineering Enterprise (electrical)	Gyo Obata, Bill Valentine, Robert Stauder, Robert L. Canfield, Ted Davalos, James E. Keller, Roger Klemm
Dallas Galleria Dallas, Texas	1983	Madeley Engineers, Inc.	I.A. Naman & Associates, Inc.	Gyo Obata, Jim Fetterman, David Suttle
King Khaled International Airport Riyadh, Saudi Arabia	1983	Bechtel Corporation	Bechtel Corporation	Gyo Obata, Bill Valentine, Frank McCurdy, Robert Stauder, Floyd Zimmerman, Janis Purgalis, Richard Quinn, Roslyn Singer Brandt, Bradley James Hill
King Saud University Riyadh, Saudi Arabia	1984	Caudill Rowlett Scott	Syska & Hennessy	Gyo Obata, Chih-Chen Jen, George Hagee, Peter Hoyt, Chester Roemer, Tad Tucker, David Cotner, James Agne, Robert Barr, Richard Tell, John Lesire, Richard Peat, Richard Lapka, Nick Ogura, David Munson, Joseph Drachnick, Floyd Zimmerman, Robert Lasky, Charles P. Reay, Debbie Fitzpatrick, Ken Hanser
Kellogg Company Corporate Headquarters Battle Creek, Michigan	1986	Gillum Consulting	HOK	Gyo Obata, David Whiteman, Richard Peat, Charles P. Reay, Peter Bobe, Jerry Sincoff
Congregation B'nai Amoona St. Louis, Missouri	1987	HOK	HOK	Gyo Obata, Jerry Sincoff, Robert Schwartz, David Chassin, Gary Goldberg
Community of Christ World Headquarters Independence, Missouri	1993	HOK	Smith & Boucher	Gyo Obata, Bob Stockdale, Charles Hook, Richard Tell, Chip Crawford, Jerry Sincoff

236

Project Name Location	Comp. Date	Structural	Mechanical/ Electrical	HOK Team
The Florida Aquarium Tampa, Florida	1995	Syska & Hennessy	Syska & Hennessy	Gyo Obata, Alan Temple, Edward Bartz, Keith Greminger, Courtney Bean Obata
Federal Reserve Bank of Minneapolis Headquarters and Operations Center Minneapolis, Minnesota	1997	Siebold Sydow & Elfanbaum, Inc.	Michaud Cooley Erickson	Gyo Obata, William Odell, Robert Edmonds, Richard Peat, David Amalong, Mark Herman, Jim Fetterman, John Lowe, Krista Kudla, David Chassin, Charles Hook, Peter Bobe, Hector Ayala, Clark Davis, Loretta Fulvio, Hung Dao, Nora Akerberg, James Adkins, Lee LeBoeuf, Tom Kaczkowski, Chip Crawford, Bob Blaha
Boeing Leadership Center St. Louis, Missouri	1999	HOK	Ross & Baruzzini, Inc.	Gyo Obata, Clark Davis, Thomas Goulden, David Buckley, Bob Blaha, Steven Crang, Sue Weist, Bob Belden, David Amalong, Margaret McDonald, Michelle Ludwig, Randy Jasper, Art Benkelman
Bristol-Myers Squibb Company Lawrenceville, New Jersey	1999	LeMessurier Associates/SCI	Joseph R. Loring & Associates	Gyo Obata, Jerry Sincoff, George Hagee, Tom Goulden, David Suttle, Mike Tatum, Dennis Cassani, Charles P. Reay
Japanese American National Museum Los Angeles, California	1999	KPFF	Hayakawa Associates	Gyo Obata, Paul Nagashima
Missouri History Museum Emerson Center St. Louis, Missouri	1999	David Mason & Associates	Parsons Brinckerhoff	Gyo Obata, Mark Husser, Robert Powers, Michael Haggans, Lyle Hodgin
Thomas F. Eagleton U.S. Courthouse St. Louis, Missouri	2000	HOK	HOK	Gyo Obata, Steven Brubaker, Bob Schwartz, Bob Stockdale, Chip Crawford, Joe Robertson, Lee LeBoeuf
Barnes-Jewish Hospital Washington University School of Medicine Center for Advanced Medicine St. Louis, Missouri	2001	EQE - THEISS	Affiliated Engineers	Gyo Obata, Hank Winkelman, Paul Strohm, David Buckley, William Burke, Nancy Coleman, Jen-shen Chan, Pete Ohlhausen, Michael Repovich, Sammy D'amico, Bruce Brunner
Alfred A. Arraj U.S. Courthouse Denver, Colorado	2002	Martin/Martin, Inc.	The RMH Group, Inc	Gyo Obata, Bob Schwartz, Mark Husser, Hans Hecker, Robert Edmonds
Obata Private Residence Ladue, Missouri	2004			Gyo Obata
Abraham Lincoln Presidential Library and Museum Springfield, Illinois	2005	Hanson Engineers Inc.	Cosentini Associates (library), EDM (museum)	Gyo Obata, Gerry Gilmore, Fred Goebel, Meera Jain, Charles Hook, Austin Hasek, Robert Edmonds, Andy Clinch, Jack Hipps, John Corson
Washington University School of Medicine, Farrell Learning and Teaching Center St. Louis, Missouri	2005	HOK	Ross & Baruzzini, Inc.	Gyo Obata, Clark Davis, William Burmeister, Thomas Polucci, James Adkins, Robert Barringer, Jen-shen Chan
Wrigley Global Innovation Center Chicago, Illinois	2005	HOK	Environmental Systems Design	Gyo Obata, Todd Halamka, Gaute Grindheim, John Hopkins
Centene Plaza Clayton, Missouri	2010	Thornton Tomasetti	ESD	Gyo Obata, Dennis Laflen, Clark Davis, Tim Gaidis, Jim Fetterman
Great American Building at Queen City Square Cincinnati, Ohio	2011	Thornton Tomasetti	Cosentini Associates	Gyo Obata, Joe Robertson, Tim Gaidis, Lee LeBoeuf, Matthew Snelling, Joe Vickery, Jason Kerensky, David Dimitry, Seth Teel

PHOTOGRAPHY AND ILLUSTRATION CREDITS

Boeing Leadership Center
Steve Hall of Hedrich Blessing (132, 134, 135, 136, 137, 138, 139, 140, 141)
HOK (133)

Bristol-Myers Squibb Company
HOK (143)
Todd Owyoung (144, 145, 146, 147, 149)
Wright (142)
George Silk (148)

Japanese American National Museum
HOK (151)
Marvin Rand (150, 152, 153, 154, 155 left, 155 right, 156, 157)

Missouri History Museum, Emerson Center
HOK (159)
Balthazar Korab (158, 163, 164)
Todd Owyoung (160, 161, 162, 165)

Thomas F. Eagleton U.S. Courthouse
Sam Fentress (170, 171)
Timothy Hursley (166, 167, 168, 169, 172, 173)

Barnes-Jewish Hospital
Washington University School of Medicine
Center for Advanced Medicine
Timothy Hursley (174, 176, 177)
Todd Owyoung (178, 179 180, 181)

Alfred A. Arraj U.S. Courthouse
Greg Hursley (182, 186)
HOK (183, 184)
McGuire Photographics (188, 189)
Frank Ooms (185, 187)

Abraham Lincoln Presidential Library and Museum
Timothy Hursley (190, 192, 193)
HOK (191)
Todd Owyoung (194, 196, 197)

Washington University School of Medicine, Farrell Learning and Teaching Center
Sam Fentress (198, 200, 201, 202, 204)
Todd Owyoung (203, 205, 206, 207)

Wrigley Global Innovation Center
Steve Hall of Hedrich Blessing (208, 210, 213, 214)
HOK (209, 211, 212, 215)

Centene Plaza
HOK (216, 217, 219, 220)

Great American Building at Queen City Square
HOK (222, 223, 224, 225, 227)

Obata Residence
Sam Fentress (228, 229, 230 top, 230 bottom, 231 top, 231 bottom)

Gyo Obata Portrait
Suzy Gorman (232)

ACKNOWLEDGEMENTS: **MARLENE ANN BIRKMAN**

Building this book took the support and talents of many. In the cornerstone, I thank my family for their love: Beverly Birkman McKendy, Tom McKendy, Ellen Ziegler Birkman, my nieces and nephews, mother, Anna, and father, Herbert. Heart-felt thanks also to: Mary Strauss, Susan Blair Bennett, Lynn and Bob Rubright, Araceli Kopiloff-Zimmer, Silvia Navia, Jeanne Fluri, Mary Krogness, Ted Green, Brian Kennelly, Debbie Stiles, Elissa Kido, Charles Parks, James Greenberg, and Jan Greenberg. My appreciation extends to Helane Rosenberg, Sarah Whitney, Joe Trimmer, Brenda Fyfe, Bradford Smart, the Bullocks, Bill Dyer, colleagues and students at Webster University, and all of my friends for their cheer and cheers. Long overdue gratitude goes to professors Barriss Mills, William Stafford, Darrel Abel and Margaret Church, and Purdue University.

Special thanks also to Gyo's clients and associates. Memories of each, daily delight and inspire me. I applaud you. And thank you to Kiku Obata and her associates, Carole Jerome and Paul Scherfling, who brought form, life, and pleasure to the project. Like her father, Kiku lives her name. And to Barbara Barrier, who while juggling so many other things, transcribed hours of tapes, I shout "bravo" for her never-wavering agility, verve, and friendship. And thank you to the late, treasured Courtney Obata, my friend, and Arlan Birkman, my brother, who served as my muses.

And most of all, I thank Gyo Obata for his everlasting spirit and patience, allowing me always to feel that he was only a stone's throw away—a Petoskey, that is. By example, Gyo taught me anew to stop, look, and listen to the promise of each day. I am ever grateful for the gift of knowing Gyo. Because of his imagination and of all those at HOK, I now look at any enclosed space, including a simple tent, with wonder.